FAMOUS COUPLES OF THE BIBLE

FAMOUS COUPLES
of the
BIBLE

♦♦♦

SECRETS FROM
BIBLE MARRIAGES

♦♦♦

Richard L. Strauss

LIVING STUDIES
Tyndale House Publishers, Inc.
Wheaton, Illinois

With grateful acknowledgment to my secretary,
Nancy Thweatt, who not only faithfully typed this
manuscript, but also contributed many of the
discussion questions at the conclusion of each
chapter.

All Scripture quotations are from the New American
Standard Bible, © The Lockman Foundation 1960,
1962, 1963, 1968, 1971, 1972, 1973, 1975, and are
used by permission.

Famous Couples of the Bible
was originally published under the title
Living in Love

Seventh printing, August 1987
Library of Congress Catalog Card Number 81-86407
ISBN 0-8423-0836-9
Copyright © 1978 by Tyndale House Publishers, Inc.,
Wheaton, Illinois

Contents

THE HONEYMOON IS OVER
The Story of Adam and Eve

HONEYMOONS are delightful times. The word itself virtually drips with the freshness and excitement of young love. The term seems to have been coined to convey the idea that the first *muum*, or first month, of marriage is the sweetest and most satisfying. But that's not exactly the way it ought to be. God would be pleased for our marriages to get better as time passes. Every new month should be sweeter and more satisfying than the one before. Unfortunately, some marriages have turned out just as the word honeymoon implies—the first month was the best, and everything has gone downhill from there. Maybe we can help reverse the trend by looking into the Word of God.

The Scripture does not specifically say so, but I have a feeling the honeymoon lasted much longer than a month for Adam and Eve.

7

Only God knows how many months or years of pure ecstasy lie between chapters two and three of Genesis. But no human relationship ever surpassed theirs in those early days for sheer joy and rapturous delight. It was, without a doubt, *the perfect marriage*.

Consider it for a moment. If ever a marriage was made in heaven, this one was. It was perfectly planned and perfectly performed by a perfect God. First he sculptured Adam (Gen. 2:7). Molded by the Master Maker, Adam doubtless had a flawless physique and ruggedly handsome features. And he was made in God's own image (Gen. 1:27). That means he had a Godlike personality—perfect intellect, emotions, and will. He possessed a brilliant mind, undiminished by sin. He had faultless emotions, including tender and totally unselfish love, the love of God himself. And he had a will that was in complete harmony with the purposes of his creator. Women, wouldn't you like to have a man like that? Physically, mentally, emotionally, and spiritually perfect!

But let me tell you about Eve. "So the Lord God caused a deep sleep to fall upon the man, and he slept; then He took one of his ribs, and closed up the flesh at that place. And the Lord God fashioned into a woman the rib which He had taken from the man, and brought her to the man" (Gen. 2:21, 22). Adam must have gazed at Eve with awe and appreciation. This was God's creative genius at its best, unblemished grace and beauty, pure loveliness of face and form. Fashioned by the hand of God himself, Eve had to be the most gorgeous creature who ever walked the face of the earth. And like Adam, she was made in God's image. Her mind, emotions, and will were unaffected by sin. What man wouldn't go for a woman like that?

Adam immediately recognized her similarity to himself. He said, "This is now bone of my bones, and flesh of my flesh; she shall be called Woman, because she was taken out of Man" (Gen. 2:23). It seems that without any special revelation from God, Adam instinctively knew that Eve was made from him; she was part of him; she was his equal;

she was his complement and counterpart. He called her woman, "female man." He drew her to himself in tender love. She ended his biting loneliness and filled his life with happiness. She was just exactly what he needed. And nothing brought her more satisfaction than the assurance that her husband needed her so very much. What intense and indescribable pleasure they found in each other's company! How they loved one another!

Their home was located in Eden, the perfect place (Gen. 2:8). The word Eden means "delight," and delightful it was. Well-watered at the fountainhead of four rivers, Eden was a luscious green paradise, blanketed with every beautiful and edible growing thing (Gen. 2:9, 10). They cultivated the ground, but as they had no thistles or weeds to contend with, their work was totally effortless and enjoyable. Side by side they lived and labored in perfect harmony, sharing a sense of mutual interdependence, enjoying a freedom of communion and communication, possessing a deep-flowing affection that bound their spirits to each other. They were inseparable.

Oh, there was an order of authority in their relationship. Adam was formed first, then Eve, as the Apostle Paul was careful to mention (1 Tim. 2:13). And Eve was made for Adam, not Adam for Eve, as Paul also pointed out (1 Cor. 11:9). But she was his *helper* (Gen. 2:18), and in order to be an effective helper she had to share all of life with him. She was with him when God issued the command to subdue the earth and have dominion over it and, consequently, she shared that awesome responsibility equally with her husband (Gen. 1:28). She did everything a helper would be expected to do. She assisted him, encouraged him, advised him, and inspired him, and she did it with a spirit of sweet submissiveness. Adam never resented her help, not even her advice. After all, that is why God gave her to him. Neither did she resent his leadership. His attitude was never tainted with superiority or exploitation. How could it be? His love was perfect. She was someone special to him and he treated her as such.

He could not give of himself enough to express his gratitude to her, and he never had a thought about what he was receiving in return. She could not possible resent leadership like that.

The Word of God says, "And the man and his wife were both naked and were not ashamed" (Gen. 2:25). It was a relationship of perfect purity and innocence. There was no sin in them. There was no strife between them. They were at peace with God, at peace with themselves, and at peace with each other. This was truly the perfect marriage. This was paradise. How we wish it would have lasted, that we could experience the same degree of marital bliss they enjoyed in those glorious days. But something happened.

The biblical account brings us, secondly, to *the entrance of sin*. There is no doubt that the subtle tempter who approached Eve in this episode was Satan using the body of a serpent as his instrument (cf. Rev. 12:9). His first approach was to question the Word of God. "Indeed, has God said, 'You shall not eat from any tree of the garden'?" (Gen. 3:1). After he questioned God's Word, he flatly denied it: "You surely shall not die!" he dogmatically declared (Gen. 3:4). Finally, he ridiculed God and brazenly distorted his Word: "For God knows that in the day you eat from it your eyes will be opened, and you will be like God, knowing good and evil" (Gen. 3:5). They would know evil all right, but they would not be as God. In reality the very opposite would be true. The likeness to God they did enjoy would be scarred and spoiled. Satan's methods have not changed much through the centuries. We know them well—the doubts, the distortions, the denials. Yet we too fall prey to them. We can identify with Eve in her moment of weakness. We know what it is to yield to temptation.

Satan used the tree of the knowledge of good and evil to do his sinister work. God had placed that tree in the garden to be the symbol of Adam and Eve's submission to him (Gen. 2:17), but Satan sometimes uses even good things to lure us from God's will. "When the woman saw

that the tree was good for food, and that it was a delight
to the eyes, and that the tree was desirable to make one
wise, she took from its fruit and ate; and she gave also to her
husband with her, and he ate" (Gen. 3:6). Have you
noticed that Eve was tempted in all three major areas listed
in 1 John 2:16? 1). The lust of the flesh—"good for food."
2). The lust of the eyes—"a delight to the eyes." 3). The
pride of life—"to make one wise." These are the same
major areas Satan uses to get us out of sorts with God and
with each other—the desire to gratify our physical senses,
the desire to have material things, and the desire to
impress people with our importance.

Instead of fleeing from temptation as the Scriptures later
exhort us to do, Eve flirted with it. She had everything a
person could want in life, but she stood there and allowed
her mind to meditate on the one thing she did not have
until it became an obsession with her and brought her
happy honeymoon to an unhappy termination. That same
kind of vicious greed has ended many a honeymoon since.
Husbands sometimes squander grocery money on
recreational equipment, hobbies, cars, or clothes. Wives
sometimes drive their husbands to make more money so
they can have bigger, better, and more expensive things.
And the material possessions of this world drive a
wedge between them. When we allow our minds to covet
material things, God calls it idolatry (Col. 3:5). And he
pleads with us to run from it: "Wherefore, my beloved,
flee from idolatry" (1 Cor. 10:14).

Eve did not flee. "She took from its fruit and ate" (Gen.
3:6). The text is not clear, but the words "gave also to
her husband with her" might imply that Adam watched her
do it. We have no idea why he did not try to stop her,
or why he did not refuse to follow her in her sin. But we do
know that he failed her woefully on this occasion. He
neglected to provide the spiritual leadership God wanted
him to provide, and instead he let her lead him into
sin. What a powerful influence a woman has over her man!
She can use it to challenge him to new heights of spiritual

accomplishment, or she can use it to drag him to depths of shame. God gave Eve to Adam to be his helper, but her covetous heart destroyed him.

Together they waited for the new delights of divine wisdom Satan had promised them. Instead, a horrid sense of guilt and shame crept over them. Their spirits died at that very moment (Gen. 2:17), and their physical bodies began the slow process of decay that would mar God's beautiful handiwork and end ultimately in physical death. The Apostle Paul was speaking of physical death when he said, "Therefore, just as through one man sin entered into the world, and death through sin, and so death spread to all men, because all sinned" (Rom. 5:12). That's the way it is with sin. It promises so much and delivers so little. It promises freedom, wisdom, and pleasure, but it delivers bondage, guilt, shame, and death.

Suddenly their nakedness became symbolic of their sin (Gen. 3:7). It exposed them openly to the penetrating eyes of the most holy God. They tried to cover their bodies with fig leaves, but it was not acceptable. God would later reveal that the only adequate covering for sin would involve the shedding of blood (Gen. 3:21; Lev. 17:11; Heb. 9:22).

That brings us, finally, to *the painful aftermath*. Sin is accompanied by disastrous consequences whether or not we are willing to accept the blame for it. Adam blamed his part of the tragedy on Eve and God: "The woman whom Thou gavest to be with me, she gave me from the tree, and I ate" (Gen. 3:12). Eve said the devil made her do it (Gen. 3:13). In much the same way, we may try to blame our marital problems on someone else. "If she would only stop nagging I could. . . ." "If he would only be more considerate I could. . . ." But God held them both responsible, just as he holds each of us responsible for our part of the blame. And there is usually some blame on both sides. God wants us to face it squarely, not skirt around it.

The consequences were almost more than Adam and Eve could bear. For Eve, the pain of childbirth would be a recurring reminder of her sin. In addition to that, she would experience an insatiable yearning for her husband, a piercing desire for his time, his attention, his affection, and his assurance. Her need would be so great, her sinful husband would seldom be willing to meet it.

And finally, the authority Adam possessed over Eve from creation was strengthened by the word *rule*. "And he shall rule over you" (Gen. 3:16). In the hands of a sinful man, that rule would degenerate at times to harsh and heartless domination over her—disregard for her feelings and disdain for her opinions. Eve no doubt chafed grudgingly under the sting of her sin as Adam drifted farther from her, paid less attention to her, and became preoccupied with other things. Bitterness, resentment, and rebellion began to settle in her soul.

For Adam, cultivating the ground became an endless, tedious chore. Anxiety over his ability to provide for his family added to his agitation and irritability and made him less sympathetic to his wife's needs. As a result, conflict entered their home. Sin always brings tension, strife, and conflict. And never was that more painfully obvious to Adam and Eve than when they stood beside the first grave in human history. Their second son had lost his life in an ugly family squabble. The honeymoon was over!

This would be the saddest story ever told were it not for a glorious ray of hope by which God illuminated the darkness. Speaking to Satan he said, "And I will put enmity between you and the woman, and between your seed and her seed; He shall bruise you on the head, and you shall bruise him on the heel" (Gen. 3:15). God promised that the seed of the woman, a child born into the human race, would destroy the works of the devil, including the havoc he had made of the home. This is the first biblical prophecy of the coming Redeemer. And now he has come! He has died for the sins of the world. His perfect blood is a satisfactory covering for the sins of every human being who will trust him. He offers to forgive us freely and restore us to his favor. And he makes available to us his

13

supernatural strength to help us live above our sin.

He can even help us overcome sin's consequences in our marital relationships. He can give husbands the same tender love and unselfish consideration that Adam had for Eve before they sinned. He can give wives the same encouraging helpfulness and sweet submissiveness that Eve had toward Adam before the Fall. In other words, the honeymoon can begin again. But we must first receive Jesus Christ as Savior from sin. There is no hope for a marital relationship to become all it can be until both husband and wife have the assurance of forgiveness and acceptance by God. That assurance can only be experienced when we have acknowledged our sin and placed our trust in Jesus Christ's perfect sacrifice on Calvary for deliverance from the eternal condemnation which our sin deserves.

If you have any doubt, settle it now. In all earnestness and sincerity, pray something like this: "Lord, I acknowledge my sin to you. I believe that Jesus Christ died to deliver me from sin's guilt, sin's penalty and sin's control of my life. I here and now place my trust in him as my personal Savior from sin and receive him into my life. Thank you, Lord Jesus, for coming into my life and forgiving my sin." When you have made that decision, the way is clear for God to fill your heart with his tenderness and love, take away your selfishness and stubbornness, and give you a self-sacrificing concern for the needs of your mate. And you may yet enjoy a little taste of paradise.

Let's talk it over.

1. Is the issue of eternal salvation firmly settled in your mind? If not, is there any good reason why you should not settle it right now?

2. What ingredients that made Adam and Eve's marriage a "honeymoon" can improve your marriage?

3. In what ways could Satan use the desire to satisfy physical needs to affect the relationship between a husband and wife

today? How about the desire for material things? the desire to be well thought of by others?

4. In what ways can a wife challenge her husband to higher goals? In what ways is it possible for a wife to weaken and destroy her husband?

5. What can husbands and wives do to help keep from blaming their problems on each other?

6. What can a husband do to meet more fully his wife's tremendous need for his attention and affection?

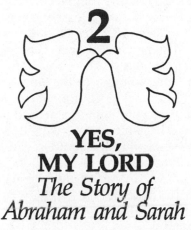

2

YES, MY LORD
The Story of Abraham and Sarah

GOD SAID to Eve, "Yet your desire shall be for your husband, and he shall rule over you" (Gen. 3:16). That was part of the burden which sin brought to the woman, and it is interesting that the next major husband and wife relationship in Scripture illustrates a wife's submission to her husband's rule. Sarah is commended twice by New Testament writers, once for her faith (Heb. 11:11) and once for her submission to her husband (1 Pet. 3:5, 6). The Apostle Peter went so far as to say she "obeyed Abraham, calling him lord."

We would not think of asking a wife to call her husband "lord" in our culture, but in that day it was Sarah's way of expressing her submissiveness. Strangely enough, these two principles, faith and submission, actually go together. Submission for a wife is basically faith that God is working through her husband to accomplish what is best for her. And that is the story of Sarah's life with Abraham.

Look first at *the early seeds of faith*. The story began in the city of Ur, a thriving metropolis near the ancient coastline of the Persian Gulf. At least one man was repulsed by the idolatry and sin of Ur, for he had come to know the one true and living God. In fact, God had spoken to him: "Go forth from your country, and from your relatives and from your father's house, to the land which I will show you; and I will make you a great nation, and I will bless you, and make your name great; and so you shall be a blessing; and I will bless those who bless you, and the one who curses you I will curse. And in you all the families of the earth shall be blessed" (Gen. 12:1-3). Armed with that potent promise, Abraham pulled up stakes, and with his father Terah, his nephew Lot, and his wife Sarah, began the long trek northward around the fertile crescent to the city of Haran.

Moving is no fun, particularly when your moving van is a camel or a donkey, and especially when you don't even know where you are going! "By faith Abraham, when he was called, obeyed by going out to a place which he was to receive for an inheritance; and he went out, not knowing where he was going" (Heb. 11:8). That is probably harder on a woman than it is on a man. Sarah is not mentioned in that verse, but her faith is there, every bit as steadfast as Abraham's. She believed that God would sustain her through the arduous journey and show her husband the place he had chosen for them.

Sarah was not a weak, spineless, overly dependent, empty-headed woman. Her parents called her *Sarai*, and names had meaning in the ancient biblical world. Hers meant "princess." It may have described her great beauty, which is referred to twice in the inspired record (Gen. 12:11, 14). It probably described, as well, her cultured upbringing, her fine education, her stately charm, and her gracious manner. When God changed her name to *Sarah*,

18

he did not remove the princely connotation, but rather added the further dignity of motherhood. She is called in that context "a mother of nations" (Gen. 17:15, 16).

Sarah was an intelligent and capable woman. But when she married Abraham she made a decision. She established as her mission in life the task of helping her husband fulfill God's purposes for him. That was not weakness. It was God's will for her life: true biblical submission. Some wives have been systematically sabotaging God's plan for their husbands because they have not been willing to believe God and entrust themselves to his wisdom. They simply will not trust God to work through their husbands to accomplish what is best. They feel they must help God along by trying to dominate their husbands.

It appears as though Abraham's father refused to go on when they reached Haran. He was an idol worshiper (Josh. 24:2), and the city of Haran suited him fine for the remainder of his days. He delayed God's purposes for Abraham, but he could not destroy them. At Terah's death, Abraham, then seventy-five years of age, departed from Haran for the land which God had promised him (Gen. 12:4). It was another move to another unknown place, but by his side was Sarah, woman of submission and faith (Gen. 12:b). The days ahead would see her faith severely tested and her submissiveness sorely tried.

Let's explore, secondly, *the continuing struggles of faith*. Faith grows best under attack. The person who prays for God to take away his problems may be asking for a sickly spiritual life. Sometimes our faith falters under the stress, but if we admit the failure and accept God's forgiveness, even those failures can contribute to our spiritual growth. Abraham and Sarah are both commended for their great faith in Scripture, but their failures are recorded for our instruction and encouragement.

The first attack came shortly after they entered Canaan. There was a famine in the land and Abraham decided to leave the place which God had promised him and flee into Egypt (Gen. 12:10). Had he consulted Sarah, she might have pointed out the foolishness of his decision, but like many men he moved ahead with his plans without considering the hardships he could cause her. Too many men refuse to ask advice from their wives. They think headship gives them the prerogative of doing whatever they please without talking it over with their wives and coming to a mutually acceptable agreement. They are afraid their wives might find cracks in their logic or expose their narrow-minded selfishness. So they barge ahead with their plans and the whole family suffers for it.

As they neared Egypt, Abraham said to his wife, "See now, I know that you are a beautiful woman; and it will come about when the Egyptians see you, that they will say, 'This is his wife'; and they will kill me, but they will let you live. Please say that you are my sister so that it may go well with me because of you, and that I may live on account of you" (Gen. 12:11-13). It was a tribute to Sarah's beauty that at sixty-five years of age she was still so irresistible that Abraham thought the Egyptians might try to kill him for her. And the beauty was not just in Abraham's eye. "And it came about when Abram came into Egypt, the Egyptians saw that the woman was very beautiful. And Pharaoh's officials saw her and praised her to Pharaoh; and the woman was taken into Pharaoh's house" (Gen. 12:14, 15). While Abraham thought the Egyptians might murder him to get his wife, he was sure they would treat him as an honored guest if they thought he were her brother. And he turned out to be right. They gave him many animals and servants for her sake (Gen. 12:16). Now technically, Sarah *was* Abraham's sister—his half-sister (Gen. 20:12). Such marriages were not unusual in that day. But what they told the Pharaoh was only a half-truth, and half-truths are lies in God's economy. He cannot honor sin.

Why did Sarah go along with his sinful scheme? Is not this a case where obedience to God would supersede obedience to one's husband? I think it is. A wife has no obligation to obey her husband when obedience compromises the clearly revealed will of God (cf. Acts 5:29). Sarah could have justly refused. But it does show how deep her faith and submission really were. Sarah believed God's promise that Abraham would become the father of a great nation. Since there were no children as yet, she was expendable, but Abraham had to live and have children even if it should be by another woman.

She may also have believed that God would intervene and deliver her before immorality became necessary. That would be quite probable in view of Pharaoh's large harem. She may likewise have believed that God would reunite her with her husband and rescue both of them from Pharaoh's power. And because she believed, she submitted. God could have protected them apart from Abraham's selfish scheme, but Sarah's faith in God and submission to her husband are still beautifully illustrated in this Old Testament narrative. The true test of a wife's submission may come when she knows her husband is making a mistake.

It is hard to imagine a man sinking much lower than Abraham did on this occasion. Even the pagan king rebuked him for what he did (Gen. 12:18-20). He failed Sarah sadly, but God was faithful to her. He honored her faith and delivered her. He never forsakes those who trust him. You would *think* the lesson of God's sovereign care would have been so indelibly inscribed on Abraham's soul after this experience that he would never compromise his wife again to protect himself. But he did. About twenty years later he did exactly the same thing with Abimelech, king of Gerar (Gen. 20:1-8). This shows how weak and faithless the faithful can be. There are probably some sins we think we will never commit again, but we must ever be watchful, for that is exactly where Satan will attack us. The amazing thing is that Sarah submitted again on that later occasion, and that God delivered her again, another evidence of her faith and God's faithfulness.

The next great strain on their faith is revealed in this statement: "Now Sarai, Abram's wife had borne him no children" (Gen. 16:1). God was soon to change Abram's name to Abraham, from "exalted father" to "father of a multitude." How could Abraham be the father of a multitude when he had no son? Now it was Sarah's turn to devise a clever human scheme. She offered her Egyptian slave girl, Hagar, so that Abraham might have a son by her. We must admit that her suggestion revealed her belief that God would keep his word and give Abraham a son. It was obviously motivated by her love for Abraham and her desire for him to have that son. And sharing her husband with another woman would have been one of the most sacrificial things she could do. But it was not God's way. It was another fleshly solution. And God's ways are always best even when he is withholding what we think we need at the moment.

Too often we time-conscious earthlings resent his long delays and take matters into our own hands, usually to our great distress. If we could learn to keep trusting him when our situation looks the bleakest, we would save ourselves much grief.

This impulsive sin had its effect on the relationship between Abraham and Sarah. Hagar got pregnant and eventually became proud and unmanageable. Sarah blamed Abraham for the whole problem when it was actually her own idea. Then she dealt harshly with Hagar, and her unkindness exposed the bitterness and resentment in her soul. Meanwhile, Abraham shirked his duty. He should have said "No" to Sarah's sinful scheme in the first place. But now he told her to handle the problem herself, to do whatever she wanted to do, but to stop badgering him about it (Gen. 16:6).

It's hard for a wife to be in subjection to a jellyfish, a man who avoids issues, puts off decisions, and shirks his responsibilities. There is nothing to submit to, no leadership to follow. A wife cannot help her husband fulfill God's goals for his life when she doesn't even know what his goals are.

Even great men and women of faith have their moments of faithlessness. And no such moment was worse for Abraham and Sarah than when they laughed at God. They both did it. God told Abraham he would bless Sarah and make her a mother of nations. Kings of peoples would come from her. Abraham fell on his face and laughed, and said, "Will a child be born to a man one hundred years old? And will Sarah, who is ninety years old, bear a child?" (Gen. 17:17). Abraham tried to get God to accept Ishmael as his heir, but God said, "No, but Sarah your wife shall bear you a son, and you shall call his name Isaac; and I will establish My covenant with him for an everlasting covenant for his descendants after him" (Gen. 17:19).

Sarah's turn was next. The Lord appeared to Abraham in the person of a visitor to his tent, and Sarah overheard him say, "I will surely return to you at this time next year; and behold, Sarah your wife shall have a son" (Gen. 18:10). She was listening at the tent door and laughed to herself, saying, "After I have become old, shall I have pleasure, my lord being old also?" (Gen. 18:12). Incidentally, this was how Peter knew she called him "lord." The submission was there, but her faith was wavering. The struggles of faith are real and we all experience them. Satan's darts of doubt seem to be flying in our direction much of the time, and we too may be tempted to snicker skeptically at the very thought of God solving our thorny problems.

But thank God for *the final triumph of faith*. I believe the turning point in their struggling faith occurred during that last encounter with the Lord. "Why did Sarah laugh?" God asked quickly. "Is anything too difficult for the Lord?" (Gen. 18:13, 14). That poignant challenge pierced their faltering hearts, and faith was rekindled, strong and steadfast. There was that brief setback in Gerar (Gen. 20:1-8). But basically things were different from that moment on.

Of Abraham, the Apostle Paul wrote, "And without

becoming weak in faith he contemplated his own body, now as good as dead since he was about a hundred years old, and the deadness of Sarah's womb; yet, with respect to the promise of God, he did not waver in unbelief, but grew strong in faith, giving glory to God, and being fully assured that what He had promised, He was able also to perform" (Rom. 4:19-21).

Of Sarah, the writer to the Hebrews declared, "By faith even Sarah herself received ability to conceive, even beyond the proper time of life, since she considered Him faithful who had promised" (Heb. 11:11). Their faith was rewarded; Sarah had a son and they called his name Isaac, which means "laughter." And Sarah told us why they gave him that name: "God has made laughter for me; everyone who hears will laugh with me" (Gen. 21:6). Her laugh of doubt had turned to a laugh of triumphant joy, and we can share her joy with her.

There would still be problems for Abraham and Sarah. The life of faith is never free from obstacles. Hagar and Ishmael were still around to poke fun at Isaac. And Sarah got upset about that. When she saw Ishmael mocking her little Isaac she seemed to lose control of herself. She rushed in to Abraham and angrily demanded, "Drive out this maid and her son, for the son of this maid shall not be an heir with my son Isaac" (Gen. 21:10). Could this be the same woman who is extolled in the New Testament for her submissiveness and obedience? Yes, it is. Healthy submission does not prohibit the expression of opinions. That is a sick submissiveness, usually motivated by a low self-esteem ("my opinions aren't worth anything"), by a fear of unpleasant circumstances ("I want peace at any price"), or by the avoidance of responsibility ("let somebody else make the decision; I don't want to get blamed").

Sarah at least said what was on her mind. And furthermore, she was right! Getting upset was not right. But Ishmael was not to be heir with Isaac, and God wanted him to leave the household. God told Abraham to

listen to Sarah and to do what she said (Gen. 21:12).
Imagine that—even though Sarah got emotional, God
wanted Abraham to heed her advice. He often wants to use
wives to correct their husbands, to advise them, to
mature them, to help them solve their problems and give
them insight. That's what helpers are for.

Some husbands make their wives feel like ignoramuses,
whose ideas are ridiculous and whose opinions are
worthless. The husband who does that is the real
ignoramus. He has missed out on God's best for him. If a
wife tells her husband there is a problem in their marriage,
God wants him to listen to her—listen to her evaluation
of the situation, listen to the changes she thinks should be
made, listen when she tries to share her feelings and
her needs—then do something constructive about it. One of
the prevalent problems in Christian marriages today is
that husbands are too proud to admit that there is anything
wrong and too stubborn to do anything about it. God may
want to enlighten them through their wives.

The bondwoman and her son were finally sent away.
Ishmael was now old enough to provide for his mother, and
God gave him expertise with the bow (Gen. 21:20).
And with that irritant removed, this happy little family
threesome enjoyed a time of unhindered faith and
fellowship. But the most severe trial to their faith was yet
to come. "Now it came about after these things, that
God tested Abraham" (Gen. 22:1). It was to be a very
unusual test. God said, "Take now your son, your only
son, whom you love, Isaac, and go to the land of Moriah;
and offer him there as a burnt offering on one of the
mountains of which I will tell you" (Gen. 22:2). Sarah's
name does not appear in this chapter and we seldom
mention her when we discuss it. But she certainly knew
what was going on. She probably helped them prepare
for the trip. She saw the wood, the fire, and the knife; she
saw her son Isaac, and she saw Abraham, a look of agony
etched on his weathered brow. But she saw no animal for

the sacrifice. Scripture says that Abraham believed that God could even raise Isaac from the dead (Heb. 11:19). Sarah must have believed that too.

She watched them disappear over the horizon, and though her motherly heart was breaking, she uttered not one word of protest. It was probably her greatest display of faith in God and submission to her husband's will and purpose. "For in this way in former times the holy women also, who hoped in God, used to adorn themselves, being submissive to their own husbands. Thus Sarah obeyed Abraham, calling him lord, and you have become her children if you do what is right without being frightened by any fear" (1 Pet. 3:5, 6). A Christian wife need not have any fear of submissiveness when her hope is in God. He will be faithful to his Word and use her obedience to accomplish what is best for her.

Sarah was one of those women whom King Lemuel spoke about, who did her husband good and not evil all the days of her life (Prov. 31:12). A woman can only be that kind of wife when she believes that nothing is too difficult for God, and when she believes that God can use even her husband's mistakes to bring glory to himself and blessing to their lives. And a man can only be worthy of such a submissive wife when he has learned to follow God's directions rather than pursue his own selfish goals. He knows he has no superiority to warrant his position of leadership. It is given to him by God. So he accepts it as a sacred trust and discharges it in full submission to his Lord and unselfish consideration for his wife and what is best for her.

Let's talk it over

1. For husbands: What are your goals in life? Have you communicated these goals to your wife?
For wives: In what ways can you help your husband fulfill God's purposes for his life?

26

2. Why should a husband seek his wife's advice in decisions that affect her?

3. In what kinds of situations does a wife usually find it most difficult to be submissive?

4. How does God expect a wife to react when she feels that her husband is out of the will of God?

5. For wives: Are there any areas of your submissiveness that are motivated by a low self-esteem, a fear of unpleasant circumstances, or the avoidance of responsibility? What should be the basis of a healthy submissiveness?

6. How do husbands sometimes use their headship role as a club to get their own way? What can they do to avoid it?

7. Since God places the husband in the headship role, what then are some obligations he has to his wife?

8. For wives: How does God want you to express your opinions and desires to your husband?
For husbands: How does God expect you to react when your wife is trying to communicate?

3

TALK TO ME
The Story of Isaac and Rebekah

GOD PROMISED Abraham he would be the
father of a great nation. In order to enjoy that
privileged position, he obviously had to have
a son, and we have traced the struggles of
faith that finally brought Abraham and Sarah
their son. His birth was the highlight of
their eventful and exciting walk with God.
What happiness Isaac brought to their home!
And he was such a good boy—dutiful,
obedient, and submissive to his parents.
Submissiveness would seem to be the only
way to explain how old Abraham could bind
the young man and lay him on the altar
of sacrifice. God substituted a ram in that
suspense-packed drama of obedience and
faith; Isaac was delivered and the three of
them were joyfully reunited as a family.

There is every indication that it was a close
family unit. They loved each other dearly.

Isaac mourning for his mother three full years after her death would be some indication of the love they felt for one another (Gen. 24:67).

With Ishmael gone, Isaac was the only child at home and his parents' lives revolved around him. He never wanted for anything. Abraham had grown to be fabulously wealthy by this time, and the record reveals that he gave it all to Isaac (Gen. 24:35, 36). Perhaps there was even a trace of smother love and overindulgence in their relationship.

It is doubtful that Abraham and Sarah realized they may have been affecting Isaac's personality and making him poor marital material by the way they were raising him. In fact, they had not even thought about marriage. They were enjoying him so much they seemed to forget that he needed a wife if they were to become the progenitors of a great nation. But after Sarah died, Abraham realized that he must take the initiative and make plans to find a mate for his son. That is not the way our children find their marriage partners, but for that time and culture it was a beautiful love story.

For Isaac and Rebekah, it was *a tender beginning*. Abraham was old when the story began. He called for his senior servant, the manager of his entire household, and said to him, "You shall not take a wife for my son from the daughters of the Canaanites, among whom I live, but you shall go to my country and to my relatives, and take a wife for my son Isaac" (Gen. 24:3, 4). The Canaanites were a vile race, cursed by God and doomed to destruction. God would not be pleased for Isaac to marry one of them. Although Abraham's relatives in northern Mesopotamia had their idols, they were at least a moral people who knew about God and respected him. And they were descendants of Shem who was blessed of God.

It was the only logical place to find a wife for Isaac. While we do not choose our children's mates for them anymore, we must teach them from their earliest days the importance of marrying believers (cf. 1 Cor. 7:39; 2 Cor. 6:14). It will help them find God's choice of a life partner

30

when the time comes for that important decision to be made.

So the old servant began the toilsome trip to the vicinity of Haran, where Abraham's brother had remained after Abraham migrated to Canaan sixty-five years earlier. Abraham had assured the servant that the angel of the Lord would go before him. With that sense of divine directon, he stopped at a well in the town of Nahor, which happened to be Abraham's brother's name. And he prayed that God would bring the right girl to that well and lead her to offer water for his camels. It was a very specific request for exactly the proper mate for Isaac. And there is a lesson in it for us. The best way for our children to find God's choice of a mate is to pray about it. They can begin as children to pray about the one whom God is preparing for them. Praying through those years will help them keep their minds on the one most important factor in their choice—the will of God.

Before the servant got to the "Amen," God had the answer on the way. Rebekah, who was the granddaughter of Abraham's brother, came out with her jar on her shoulder. Scripture says she was very beautiful, and a virgin. When she came from the well with her jar filled with water, the servant ran to meet her and said, "Please let me drink a little water from your jar." She said, "Drink, my lord" and she quickly gave him a drink. When he finished drinking she said, "I will draw also for your camels until they have finished drinking." So she emptied her jar into the drinking trough and ran back to the well for some more, and she drew enough water for all ten of his camels (Gen. 24:15-20).

What a girl she was—beautiful, vivacious, friendly, outgoing, unselfish, and energetic. And when the servant found out that she was the granddaughter of Abraham's brother, he bowed his head and worshiped the Lord: "Blessed be the Lord, the God of my master Abraham, who has not forsaken His lovingkindness and His truth toward my master; as for me, the Lord has guided me in the way to the house of my master's brothers" (Gen. 24:27).

It becomes obvious from the outset of this story that God is the real matchmaker in the marriage. When the servant related to Rebekah's family the indications of God's guidance, her brother and her father agreed. "The matter comes from the Lord," they said (Gen. 24:50). No matter what kinds of problems a marriage may encounter, they will be easier to solve if both husband and wife have a settled assurance that God has brought them together. Difficulties can be overcome without it, and must be if God is to be glorified. But the nagging notion that they married out of the will of God will make them less than enthusiastic about working at their relationship with self-sacrificing diligence.

Rebekah faced an immense decision in her life—leaving the home and family she would never see again, traveling nearly five hundred miles on camelback with a total stranger, to marry a man she had never met. Her family called her in and said, " 'Will you go with this man?' And she said, 'I will go' " (Gen. 24:58). It was her assurance of God's sovereign direction that motivated her decision, and it revealed her courage and trust.

Certainly the hours of travel were filled with talk of Isaac. The old servant described him honestly and completely. Isaac was an unassuming, mild-mannered, peace-loving man. He would go to any lengths to avoid a fight (cf. Gen. 26:18-25). He was also a meditative man, not a quick thinker, but rather quiet and reserved. He was not the great man his father was, but he was a good man, with a steadfast faith in God and a sense of divine mission. He knew that through his seed God would bring spiritual blessing to the whole earth (Gen. 26:3-5). He was different from the radiant, quick-witted Rebekah—far different. But the experts tell us that opposites attract. And Rebekah could feel her heart being drawn to this one whom she would soon meet and give herself to in marriage.

Isaac was out in the field meditating at evening time when the camel caravan approached carrying his precious cargo. Rebekah dismounted from the camel when she saw Isaac, and covered herself with a veil as the custom was. After he had heard all the exciting details of the eventful trip and the providential guidance that had found him a bride, we read, "Then Isaac brought her into his mother Sarah's tent, and he took Rebekah, and she became his wife; and he loved her; thus Isaac was comforted after his mother's death" (Gen. 24:67). It was a tender beginning.

But somewhere along the way, this marriage began to sour. Look, secondly, at *the tragic decline* in their relationship. We are not absolutely certain what the problem was. It certainly was not lack of love, for Isaac truly loved Rebekah, and unlike some husbands, he openly showed it. About forty years after they were married he was seen tenderly caressing her in public (Gen. 26:8). That might lead us to believe that they had a good physical relationship. And that is important to a marriage. But a husband and wife cannot spend all their time in bed. They must also build a deep and intimate communion of soul and spirit. They must honestly share what is going on inside of them, what they are thinking and feeling. And there is not much evidence that Isaac and Rebekah did that.

One problem may have been their lack of children. Isaac could have resented that and yet not ever admitted it. Having children was far more important in that day than it is today, and they tried for about twenty years without success. Much bitterness can build inside of a person in twenty years. But Isaac finally turned to the right place with his problem. "And Isaac prayed to the Lord on behalf of his wife, because she was barren; and the Lord answered him and Rebekah his wife conceived" (Gen. 25:21).

Having babies does not solve problems, however. The twins who would soon be born were only going to agitate a problem that already existed in their relationship. It seems to have been a problem of communication. Rebekah with her bubbling personality loved to talk. Isaac with his retiring personality preferred solitude and silence. He was so hard to talk to. They shared less and less with each other through those years. And Rebekah's bitterness grew because of that lack of communion and companionship for which every woman longs. Her voice probably took on a caustic tone. Her face may have developed lines of disgust and disdain. And her scornful glances and spiteful comments only drove Isaac farther from her to find his precious peace. He may even have become tone deaf to the frequency of her voice. Modern experts tells us that it can actually happen.

When Rebekah conceived, she had a violent pregnancy. Isaac was little help to her, so she cried out to the Lord for answers, and he spoke to her: "Two nations are in your womb; and two peoples shall be separated from your body; and one people shall be stronger than the other; and the older shall serve the younger" (Gen. 25:23). There is not one hint in Scripture that she ever shared with her husband this unusual divine prophecy that Jacob, the younger, would receive the blessing of the firstborn. In the only mention of Rebekah's name outside the Book of Genesis, that promise is still exclusively hers. "It was said to her, 'The older will serve the younger' " (Rom. 9:12). Why couldn't she tell him even this amazing word from God? Why was it so hard for her to talk to Isaac about anything?

Marriage counselors estimate that fully half of all their cases involve a silent husband. In some instances, like Isaac's, it may be genuinely difficult for the husband to talk. Maybe he does not think very deeply and does not have much to say. Maybe he has always been quiet and does not know how to communicate. In other instances, a normally communicative man may neglect sharing things with his wife because he gets preoccupied with other things and does not realize how important it is to talk to her. If she nags him about it, he may build a protective shroud of silence around himself and withdraw even more.

But whatever the cause of his quietness, he needs to work at communicating. His wife needs that verbal communion and companionship. God made her that way. And God can help a husband improve in this area if he wants to be helped and seeks that help from above. Whether or not he ever becomes a great talker, he can learn to be a good listener. His wife needs him to listen with undivided attention, not one ear on television and the other on her, but both ears aimed in her direction and wide open. That may be all she is really asking for. Men, love enough to listen!

There may be some cases where the problem is reversed. The husband may like to talk and the wife finds it difficult to communicate. Whichever the situation may be in your house, you can make it easier for your mate to talk by remembering a few simple principles. For one thing, don't push; let your mate choose the time he feels most free to talk. Accept him without judgment when he does express his feelings and frustrations. When you must disagree, do it kindly and respectfully, not sarcastically or condemningly. Try to understand the other person instead of trying only to be understood. Don't jump to conclusions, but patiently hear him out. And by all means, don't nag! Nagging is the world's number one communication killer.

Evidently, nobody ever told Isaac and Rebekah these things. Their relationship went from bad to worse. When the twins were born, as we might expect, their personalities were vastly different from each other. Scripture says, "When the boys grew up, Esau became a skillful hunter, a man of the field; but Jacob was a peaceful man, living in tents" (Gen. 25:27). As often happens when a husband and wife have a poor relationship with each other, Isaac and Rebekah each latched onto one of the children in a substitute relationship in order to fill the emptiness in their souls. "Now Isaac loved Esau, because he had a taste for game; but Rebekah loved Jacob" (Gen. 25:28).

Isaac saw in Esau the rugged outdoorsman that he himself never was, and he learned to enjoy Esau's sporting exploits vicariously as he savored his delicious venison stew. Rebekah, on the other hand, favored Jacob. He stayed close to home. He probably talked to her, listened to her, and helped her with her chores. And she found with him the companionship she never enjoyed with her husband. It was a pathetic arrangement, and it was bound to have serious repercussions in the lives of the boys.

Psychologists today warn us of the same two problems that were present in this ancient home. They tell us that a dominant mother and a passive father have a tendency to produce problem children, and that favoritism in the family unit tends to cause serious personality defects in the children. While a child may be getting pampered and overindulged by one parent, he is getting criticized and rejected by the other. Neither one does him any good, and both together contribute to low self-esteem and ambivalent feelings that confuse him and burden him with guilt. He grows to disrespect the parent who indulges him and despise the parent who rejects him. Ultimately he may spurn both of them and begin grasping for what he wants from life regardless of whom he hurts in the process.

That is exactly what was happening in the home of Isaac and Rebekah. Jacob showed his self-seeking grasping by stealing his brother's birthright (Gen. 25:29-34). Esau showed his contempt for his parents by marrying two Hittite women against his parents' wishes (Gen. 26:34, 35). And peace-loving Isaac sat around eating his venison stew, letting it all happen.

The tragic decline in this relationship was followed, finally, by *the treacherous end*. "Treacherous" is the best word I can think of to describe the events recorded in Genesis 27. Rebekah, eavesdropping outside the tent, heard old Isaac tell Esau to hunt some venison and make him a savory stew so that he could gain the strength to bless him before he died. Actually Isaac lived for many years after that, but he had become withdrawn and self-absorbed, approaching a state of hypochondria.

It is important to understand that he still did not know that Jacob was supposed to receive the blessing of the firstborn and become the spiritual leader of the family. Scripture later declares, "By faith Isaac blessed Jacob and Esau, even regarding things to come" (Heb. 11:20). Isaac thought he was blessing Esau, not Jacob. The Spirit of God certainly would not have said "by faith" if Isaac had given that blessing in conscious disobedience to the known will of God. Isaac still did not know!

This would have been the perfect time for Rebekah to flee to God in prayer for divine wisdom, then go in and tactfully share with Isaac the promise God had made to her shortly before the twins were born. If ever there was a time to talk it over, this was it. Had she reasoned with him lovingly on the basis of God's word to her, she certainly could have secured for Jacob the blessing God wanted him to have. But instead of prayer and reason, she chose treachery and deceit.

Concealing one's true thoughts and feelings can actually be a form of deception, and deception had become a way of life for Isaac and Rebekah. Now it was about to come into full bloom. It would be wise for us to notice this carefully, for this is the kind of thing that a lack of communication can eventually lead to.

Rebekah's diabolical plan was to help Jacob impersonate Esau so that blind old Isaac would be fooled into blessing him instead of his brother. Jacob did not like the idea because Esau was a hairy man and he was smooth. It was likely that his dad would put his hands on him, feel his smooth skin, and his deceit would be exposed, bringing him a curse rather than a blessing. But Rebekah offered to assume any curse upon herself and urged him to go ahead and do as she said. Her offer sounded so sacrificial, but it was sinful and sick.

Trust is essential to any loving relationship, and trust cannot flourish in a home where there is dishonesty and deceit as there was in this one. Husbands and wives who purposely keep things from each other, who sneak around to hide the truth about finances, the activities they are involved in, the things the children have done, or anything else, can never enjoy the fullness of God's love in their relationship. Love can only grow in an atmosphere of honesty. Peter exhorts us to lay aside all guile and hypocrisy (1 Pet. 2:1). Paul tells us to speak the truth in love (Eph. 4:15).

Rebekah and Jacob had forgotten what truth was. With the help of some goat skins, the two tricksters pulled off their deceitful plot. Isaac trembled when he later discovered that he had been victimized by his wife and son, but he would not reverse the blessing. He had blessed Jacob, "and he shall be blessed," he confidently affirmed (Gen. 27:33). Isaac realized that God had overruled his original intentions even though it was by an act of deceit. His willingness to accept it from God was such a significant expression of *faith* in God's sovereign control of his circumstances that it earned him mention in faith's hall of fame (Heb. 11:20).

Esau did not have that much faith, however. He vowed to kill his brother. But as we might expect, Rebekah came up with another ingenious idea. When she heard what Esau intended to do, she called Jacob in and said to him, "Behold your brother Esau is consoling himself concerning you, by planning to kill you. Now therefore, my son, obey my voice, and arise, flee to Haran, to my brother Laban! And stay with him a few days, until your brother's fury subsides, until your brother's anger against you subsides, and he forgets what you did to him. Then I shall send and get you from there. Why should I be bereaved of you both in one day?" (Gen. 27:42-45).

In order to get Isaac to agree to her plan, she had to deceive him again. It was another masterful performance. You can almost feel the melodrama as she exclaims, "I am tired of living because of the daughters of Heth; if Jacob takes a wife from the daughters of Heth, like these, from the daughters of the land, what good will my life be to me?" (Gen. 27:46). So Isaac dutifully called Jacob in and instructed him to go to Haran to find a wife. One deception usually does demand another, until the life of the deceiver is a hopeless web of despair.

Poor Rebekah. She thought she was doing what was right, but God never asks us to sin in order to accomplish his will. By her deception, Rebekah further alienated her husband from her; she enraged and totally estranged her firstborn son; and while she thought her beloved Jacob would be gone a few days, she never saw him again. When he returned home twenty years later, Isaac was still alive, but Rebekah lay next to Abraham and Sarah in the sepulcher cave of Machpelah.

Some of the details may vary, but the general pattern of their lives has been repeated in many homes since. Maybe it is being reenacted in yours right now. Communication is at a standstill. You live under the same roof, but you live in your own world, alone. It does not matter who is most at fault, husband or wife. Stop drifting apart; turn around and say, "I need you. I need you to talk to me. I need to know what you think and how you feel. Please share yourself with me. I need you to listen to me and to try to understand." Then start talking about it openly and honestly. Reach deep down inside of you and share with each other your hurts, your fears, your struggles, your frustrations, your weaknesses, your confusion, your needs, as well as your goals and aspirations. Then listen to one another, patiently, understandingly, and forgivingly, and encourage each other lovingly. New joys will open to you as you grow together.

Let's talk it over

1. Is there any indication of the same kind of "smother love" in your relationship with your children that caused such unhappy consequences in Isaac's marriage? What can you do about it?

2. In what ways can you teach your children the importance of marrying a believer and of seeking God's will in their choice?

3. Why do you think Rebekah never told Isaac about God's promise concerning their sons?

4. Why do husbands and wives in our day sometimes keep things from each other? What can be done to remedy the situation?

5. Do you feel you can openly share your innermost feelings with your mate? If not, why? Talk over these reasons with your mate.

6. Is what your mate shares with you of great importance to you? Do you really listen? How can you correct any shortcoming in this area?

7. What specific things can you do to encourage more open communication and more intimate communion with each other?

8. Are you sensitive to your mate's needs or do your thoughts generally dwell on how you can best be served? How can you avoid a selfish desire to have your own needs met and dwell instead on the needs of your mate?

9. How do people sometimes use their relationship with their children as a substitute for a good relationship with their mates? What are the underlying reasons for this and how can it be corrected?

4

NEVER SATISFIED!
The Story of Jacob and Rachel

WHEN WE LAST SAW Jacob he was running
from Beersheba for his life, fleeing the
vengeance of his brother Esau. He did not get
very far before he learned that God was
going with him. The message came in the
form of a dream about a ladder that stretched
from heaven to earth. The Lord stood above
the ladder and said to Jacob, "Behold, I am
with you, and will keep you wherever you
go, and will bring you back to this land; for I
will not leave you until I have done what
I have promised you" (Gen. 28:15). Jacob
called the name of the place Bethel, meaning
"house of God."

Armed with that precious promise of God's
presence, Jacob headed for Haran, the land of
his mother's family. It was a long and
lonely journey. He arrived in the general
vicinity of the city weary, footsore, homesick,

41

and not exactly sure where to go. He spotted a well and stopped to rest. There were some shepherds sitting around the well, so Jacob started a conversation with them: "My brothers, where are you from?" They answered, "We are from Haran." Jacob probably heaved a sigh of relief. The Lord had brought him safely to his destination. He continued, "Do you know Laban the son of Nahor?" "We know him," they said. Again his heart must have leaped within him at the realization of God's faithful direction. "Is it well with him?" he questioned. And they replied, "It is well, and behold, Rachel his daughter is coming with the sheep" (Gen. 29:4-6).

Jacob turned his head, took one fateful look, and it was without a doubt *love at first sight*. She was a lovely girl, "beautiful of form and face" (Gen. 29:17). And her eyes—what gorgeous eyes they were! Since they are contrasted with her older sister Leah's, which had no brightness or sparkle, they must have been dark and lustrous, captivatingly beautiful.

Jacob was impressed—probably too impressed. We get the idea that he was so fascinated by Rachel's beauty, and so enchanted by her charm, that he failed to recognize her shortcomings or even to consider the will of God in his relationship with her. And being the shrewd operator that he was, he got down to business immediately. He reminded the shepherds that grazing time was being lost and that they should water their flocks and get them back out to pasture while it was still light, probably a ploy to get rid of them so he could talk to Rachel alone. But the shepherds had some sort of agreement that they would not roll the stone back from the mouth of the well until everybody's flocks were gathered (Gen. 29:7, 8).

"While he was still speaking with them, Rachel came with her father's sheep, for she was a shepherdess. And it came about, when Jacob saw Rachel the daughter of Laban his mother's brother, and the sheep of Laban his mother's brother, that Jacob went up, and rolled the stone from the mouth of the well, and watered the flock of Laban his mother's brother" (Gen. 29:9, 10). Jacob may have been a homebody, but he was no weakling. He moved a stone that normally took several people to move, and watered all of Rachel's sheep. Could he have been showing off just a little?

We go on to read, "Then Jacob kissed Rachel, and lifted his voice and wept" (Gen. 29:11). The emotion of the moment overwhelmed him. The miracle of God's guidance and care, the thrill of meeting his pretty cousin, the prospect of what the future would hold—all of it filled his heart so full that he wept for joy. Our culture frowns on a man expressing his emotions like this, but honestly expressing one's feelings might promote greater emotional health and greater marital stability.

It seems as though this romance was off to a blazing start. The neighborhood beauty and the new boy in town had found each other. But from the beginning we are a little dubious about the match. We know that a relationship based primarily on physical attraction rests on a shaky foundation. Hollywood has given us some good evidence for that thesis. And the marital misfortunes of the proverbial football hero and homecoming queen bear it out too. They can make their marriage succeed, but it will take a little extra effort, and they will need to make their relationship grow far beyond the physical magnetism that got it started.

But when a man is enamored of a woman, he does not want to hear those things. He is going to have her, and nothing else matters. It was only one month after Jacob arrived in Haran that Uncle Laban approached him to see if they could work out a mutually acceptable wage arrangement. The Scripture says that Jacob loved Rachel and offered to serve Laban seven years for her hand in marriage (Gen. 29:18). He had nothing to offer Laban for his daughter, so his labor was promised in lieu of a dowry. Now we are even more dubious. One month is hardly sufficient time for us to get to know someone well enough to make a lifelong commitment, and it surely is not enough time to learn whether or not we are in love. True love requires thorough knowledge. To profess to love someone we do not know intimately is merely to love our mental image of that person. And if he does not measure up to our mental image, then our so-called "love" turns to disillusionment and resentment, and sometimes to hatred.

But Jacob thought he was in love. When Rachel was near, his heart pounded faster and a wonderful feeling swept over him. She was the most beautiful creature he had ever laid eyes on, and he felt life without her would be worthless. That was enough for him. "So Jacob served seven years for Rachel and they seemed to him but a few days because of his love for her" (Gen. 29:20). That is a remarkable statement. In fact, they are about the loveliest words ever penned of a man's feeling for a woman. Seven years is a long time to wait, and I think Jacob really did grow to love Rachel during those years. The physical attraction was still there, but he could not live in such close contact with her through a seven-year engagement period and not learn a great deal about her, both good and bad. This marriage was to see hard times, but had it not been for this long engagement and Jacob's deepening and maturing love, it probably would not have survived at all.

Too many couples marry in haste and repent at leisure. Seven-year engagements may be a little excessive, but *time* is needed to learn someone's desirable and undesirable traits, so that we can decide whether we can give of ourselves unselfishly for the other person's good in spite of his unappealing characteristics. One great test of true love, therefore, is the ability to wait. Infatuation is usually in a hurry because it is self-centered. It says, "I feel good when I am with you, so I want to hurry up and get you to the altar before I lose you and lose these good feelings." Love says, "Your happiness is what I want most of all, and I am willing to wait, if need be, to be sure this is what is best for you." And if it is real, it will stand the test of time. Jacob waited, and his romantic love at first sight grew to become a deep bond of spirit and a total commitment of soul.

There is an old saying that goes, "True love never runs

smoothly." That's the way it was with Jacob and Rachel. Let's look at *love under great stress*. Uncle Laban was the one who threw the monkey wrench into the machinery. Sly, deceitful old trickster that he was, he substituted Leah for Rachel on Jacob's wedding night. With a heavy veil over her face and long flowing garments covering her body, she got through the ceremony undetected. By talking in whispered tones in the darkened tent, she made it through the night. But can you imagine Jacob's utter consternation when the morning light exposed Laban's chicanery? He was probably furious with the whole family for their double-dealing fraud.

That was not exactly the happiest way for Leah to start her married life, was it? I suspect that she loved Jacob from the start and longed for him to return her affection. She cooperated willingly with her father's scheme but found very little satisfaction in the husband she had gained by deceit. Tricking someone into marriage is dangerous business, but it is still being done today. Some women try to buy a man with sex, or trap him with a baby, or lure him with family fortune. A man may also trap a woman by promising wealth, or trick a woman by pretending to be something he is not, masking his faults until after the ceremony. It may not take any longer than the honeymoon for his wife to discover that she married a monster she never really knew. The consequences of deception are usually painful and distressing.

Big-hearted Laban offered to give Rachel to Jacob as well if he would work for seven more years. "Complete the bridal week of this one, and we will give you the other also for the service which you shall serve with me for another seven years" (Gen. 29:27). The week refers to the week of wedding festivities. Jacob did not have to wait seven more years for Rachel, only one week. But he had to work seven more years without pay after marrying her. "So Jacob went in to Rachel also, and indeed he loved Rachel more than Leah, and he served with Laban for another seven years" (Gen. 29:30).

So we have the first of the God-fearing patriarchs entering into a bigamous relationship. It was not God's perfect will. God made one woman for one man (Gen. 2:24; cf. also Lev. 18:18; 1 Tim. 3:2). Although Jacob was tricked into it, there were alternatives. Some commentators insist that he should have rejected Leah since he did not take her willingly. May I suggest another alternative; Jacob could have accepted his marriage to Leah as the will of God for his life and learned to love her alone. Jacob's father accepted the consequences of his deceit when he impersonated his brother Esau and stole the family blessing, and Isaac was commended for it in the New Testament. Maybe Jacob would have been commended for accepting these consequences from the sovereign hand of God had he exercised that degree of faith. And may I remind you that Leah, not Rachel, was the mother of Judah, through whom the Savior would ultimately come (Gen. 29:35). But Jacob was not willing to believe that God was in control of these circumstances. He was going to have what he wanted in spite of God's will. And the events that follow should be evidence enough that bigamy was never part of God's plan for the human race.

In the pressure of that bigamous relationship, Rachel's true character began to surface. When she realized that Leah was bearing Jacob children and she was not, she became intensely jealous of her sister and said to Jacob, "Give me children, or else I die" (Gen. 30:1). She was saying essentially, "If I can't have my own way, I'd rather be dead." Here was a woman who had almost everything in life—great physical beauty, all the material things she needed, and the adoring devotion of a loving husband. Wasn't Jacob's love worth more than any number of sons? No, it wasn't, not for Rachel. She had to have everything she wanted or life was not worth living. She was envious, selfish, peevish, fretful, discontented, and demanding. And Jacob lost his cool. "Then Jacob's anger burned against Rachel, and he said, 'Am I in the place of God, who has withheld from you the fruit of the womb?' " (Gen. 30:2).

His anger was not right in God's sight, but his evaluation of the situation surely was. The miracle of conception lies within the power of God.

The sin of discontentment has ruined countless relationships since Jacob's day. Some couples get angry with God for not giving them children, while others who do have children look forward to the day when the kids will be grown and gone and they can have some peace and quiet. Homemakers want to be working wives, and working wives want to be full-time homemakers. There are Christians who are dissatisfied with the places where they live, the jobs they have, the money they make, and the houses they live in. Something else always looks better to them. Some wives are discontented with their husbands. They whine and scold because the men don't pay enough attention to them, don't spend enough time with the children, won't do little jobs around the house, stay out too late, or think more of their jobs, their cars, their hobbies, television, or sports than they think of them. Some husbands are discontented with their wives. They criticize them for the way they dress, the way they fix their hair, the way they cook, the way they keep house, or the way they treat the children. They get upset because they sleep too late, eat too much, waste too much time, or spend too much money. No matter how hard some wives try, they can never please their husbands.

Some of these things are important and need to be talked out. I am not suggesting that we totally ignore them and suffer in silence. But a spirit of discontent that causes us to fuss, nag, bicker, quarrel, and complain is a great hindrance to happy marital relationships. God wants us to be content with what we have. "But godliness actually is a means of great gain, when accompanied by contentment" (1 Tim. 6:6). Paul could say, "For I have learned to be content in whatever circumstances I am" (Phil. 4:11). When we can recognize the presence of discontentment in our lives and acknowledge it as sin, we can seek God's grace to overcome it and find new joy in living.

Rachel's discontentment led her to the same kind of fleshly scheme Sarah tried. She gave her handmaid Bilhah to Jacob so that he could have a son by her, and she did it twice (30:3-8). Technically, the children of that union would be Rachel's children in their culture. But we get another glimpse into Rachel's selfish nature when Bilhah's second son is born. She said, "With mighty wrestlings I have wrestled with my sister, and I have indeed prevailed" (Gen. 30:8). She named the child Naphtali, which means "wrestling." She saw herself in a contest with her sister for first place in Jacob's estimation.

Her jealous malcontent was seen again a short time later. Little Reuben, Leah's firstborn, who may have been about four years old at the time, was out in the field following the reapers around picking some plants called mandrakes or love apples, as any little boy of that time might do. When he brought them home and presented them to his mother, Rachel saw them and decided she wanted some too. She always seemed to want what somebody else had. So she peddled Jacob's affections to Leah for the night for a couple of those love apples (Gen. 30:14, 15).

The same spirit of discontent shows up again in her life. God finally did give her a son of her own, and now we expect her to be satisfied. But she named him Joseph, which means "may he add." And she said, "May the Lord give me another son" (Gen. 30:24). More, more, more! Rachel was never completely happy with what she had.

But the end is not yet. God told Jacob that it was time to leave Uncle Laban and go back home to Canaan. He had prospered to such an extent that Laban no longer felt very kindly toward him. So Jacob gathered his wives and children and his belongings and he slipped away while Laban was out shearing his sheep. But Rachel took something that did not belong to any of them; she took her father's idols, the household gods called terephim (Gen. 31:19). The possessor of those images was accepted as the principal heir of the family, even if he was only a son-in-law.

Again, Rachel's greed was showing. She wanted her husband rather than her brothers to have the largest share of the family inheritance so she could benefit from it too. When Laban finally overtook them and searched their belongings for his terephim, Rachel lied to him and deceived him to keep him from finding them (Gen. 31:33-35). This lovely little Rachel seems to have been a shrew!

But do you know what? Except for the one time that Jacob got angry with her for blaming her childlessness on him, there is no indication that he ever loved her any less for her faults. In fact, there are indications that he maintained his devotion to her to the very end of her life. For example, he put her in the favored position to the rear of the company when they went to meet Esau and their lives may have been in danger (Gen. 33:2). Jacob was far from perfect, but he is an example to us of how a husband ought to treat his wife when she isn't all that she ought to be.

Some husbands say, "I could love her more if she would only be sweet." Love that functions only when she is sweet is not really love. God wants wives to sense their husbands' intense love for them even when they are acting like stinkers (Eph. 5:25). And most of us have moments like that. Maybe men should ask themselves this question periodically, especially in the middle of a disagreement, "Is my wife conscious of my love right now? Is she feeling love, or is she feeling anger, hostility, and rejection?" God made a wife with the need to rest secure in her husband's love at all times. And that will depend largely on the attitude her husband projects by things as little as the look on his face and the tone of his voice, especially when she is moody and disagreeable.

We have seen Jacob's love at first sight and his love under great stress. Look, finally, at *love through deep sorrow*. God allowed Rachel to have her one last request. She did bear another son. Her labor was severe, and it became evident that she was going to die in childbirth. When the midwife told her she had given birth to a son, she gasped out his name with her last breath—Ben-oni, which means "Son of my sorrow." Jacob later changed it to Benjamin, "Son of my right hand." But isn't it ironic? One day years before she had screamed, "Give me children, or else I die." And she died giving birth to her second son. The child lived. But they buried Rachel by the side of the road leading from Bethlehem to Jerusalem. You can still visit her tomb today, a lasting monument to the disaster of discontentment.

Jacob never got over Rachel. At 147 years of age he called his sons together in Egypt to bless them, and he was still thinking about her. "Now as for me, when I came from Paddan, Rachel died, to my sorrow, in the land of Canaan on the journey, when there was still some distance to go to Ephrath; and I buried her there on the way to Ephrath (that is, Bethlehem)" (Gen. 48:7). He loved her to the end of his life. But what good did it do her? She could not fully enjoy his love. That gnawing discontentment kept her from enjoying anything totally, and it kept others from enjoying her. It isolated her in a grim world of loneliness. Then she died, leaving Jacob to the sister she envied so much in life. And even in death, she was alone. At Jacob's request, they buried him next to Leah in the cave of Machpelah in Hebron beside Abraham, Sarah, Isaac, and Rebekah (Gen. 49:29-31; 50:13). Rachel lies alone.

Could it be that the loneliness in our lives or the conflicts in our relationships are the result of an underlying spirit of discontentment? It will not change as long as we think satisfaction can be found in any material possession or improved circumstance. Rachel proved that. Real satisfaction can only be found in the Lord. He is the one who satisfies the thirsty soul and fills the hungry soul with good things (Ps. 107:9). He has instructed us to be content with what we have, for while the circumstances of life change daily, he is unchanging and ever with us (Heb. 13:5). As our knowledge of him increases through the study of his Word and through prayerful periods in his presence, we shall find a settled peace and contentment growing within us. Then we shall be able to receive with gratitude what he gives us, and at the same time thank him for what he denies us, being confident that his ways are perfect. And we shall be able to change what can be changed, while joyfully accepting what cannot be changed, being assured that it is part of his perfect plan to bring us to maturity in Christ.

Let's talk it over

1. Discuss some of the values of a lengthy and close acquaintance before marriage. How can couples who married without it now compensate for it?

2. What could Rachel have done to overcome her jealous discontentment? What could Jacob have done to help her?

3. What are the things in your life you would consider of the greatest value?

4. Finish the following statement as you might have done before reading this chapter: "I could be happy if only . . . ."

5. If you inserted some improved circumstance or material possession, how might you finish the statement to be more consistent with the principles of God's Word?

6. What characteristics in your mate bring you the greatest contentment? What characteristics bother you the most? If you feel that certain things should be changed, what should you do?

7. Do you feel jealousy toward some other person? How does God want you to handle those feelings?

8. For husbands: Does your wife continually sense your love for her? You might find out by asking her. How can you demonstrate love even in her "bad moments"?

TWO TO GET READY
The Story of Boaz and Ruth

IT HAD BEEN more than 500 years since they laid old Jacob to rest in the cave of Machpelah. They were eventful years for Jacob's descendants. There were the hard years of Egyptian bondage culminated by God's gracious deliverance; there were the forty years of wilderness wanderings culminated by the great conquest of Canaan; then there were the strange cyclic years of sin, servitude, and salvation we know as the period of the Judges. That gloomy era provides the setting for the most beautiful love story in the Bible, the story of Boaz and Ruth.

"Now it came about in the days when the judges governed, that there was a famine in the land. And a certain man of Bethlehem in Judah went to sojourn in the land of Moab with his wife and his two sons" (Ruth 1:1). That man, named Elimelech, died in Moab, leaving his wife, Naomi, and their two sons, Mahlon and Chilion. The boys married Moabite women, and then, in what seemed to be a tragic twist of fate, both of them died, leaving Naomi in a strange land with only her two Moabite daughters-in-law, Ruth and Orpah. When she heard that God had prospered her people with food, she decided to return home to Bethlehem.

Orpah remained in Moab at Naomi's suggestion, but Ruth would not hear of it. She was one of those rare persons who loved deeply and selflessly, and she loved her mother-in-law. Remember her famous words? "Do not urge me to leave you or turn back from following you; for where you go, I will go, and where you lodge, I will lodge. Your people shall be my people, and your God, my God" (Ruth 1:16). Her God was about to direct her to a wonderful man with whom she would be united.

The first thing that strikes us about these two whom God brought together by his grace is *their spiritual preparation*. Although Elimelech's family was out of the center of God's will and out of the place of God's blessing, they did accomplish something worthwhile. Through their testimony, this young Moabite named Ruth turned from worshiping Chemosh, the God of the Moabites, with all the abominable practices associated with his worship, and put her trust in the one true and living God. "Your God shall be my God," she boldly declared. And it was evident to all who knew her that she had come to enjoy an intimate relationship with the Lord God of Israel. Sometime later, Boaz would say to her, "May the Lord reward your work, and your wages be full from the Lord, the God of Israel, under whose wings you have come to seek refuge" (Ruth 2:12). Her trust in God and her love for God were the sources of an inner strength and beauty that could not be hidden and of a love for others that could not be suppressed.

Consider what she did. Instead of brooding over the loss of her own husband, she devoted herself to meeting the needs of her mother-in-law, to filling the void in Naomi's

life, to helping her the best she could. That meant leaving
her home, her family, and her friends, moving to another
land as a despised foreigner and living in poverty and
privation. And for what? Love and concern for her
mother-in-law were her only apparent motives. Boaz
pointed that out later in the story: "All that you have done
for your mother-in-law after the death of your husband
has been fully reported to me, and how you left your father
and your mother and the land of your birth, and came to
a people that you did not previously know" (Ruth 2:11).

Many a woman who loves her husband cannot seem to
love his mother. And men seem to have the same problem
with their wives' mothers, as evidenced by the
mother-in-law jokes that have circulated through the years.
Where does love like Ruth's come from? It comes from the
Lord of all love. If you want some of it, you will have to
cultivate a close personal relationship with him just as Ruth
did. When we get to know God and understand how much
he gave for us, we are encouraged to give of ourselves for
the good of others, even our in-laws. And when we do that,
tension and turmoil begin to dissolve into harmony and
happiness.

It is never too soon to learn these lessons of love. We can
begin teaching them to our children very early in their lives.
The training ground for love is the home. A loving
relationship with parents and brothers and sisters will
prepare them to love their mates and their mates' parents as
they should. Some folks who are reading this chapter may
have come from unloving homes and they are finding their
early influences hard to overcome. It is difficult for them to
give or to receive love. They can testify to the importance
of parents setting a loving example, then teaching their
children to be helpful and good-natured and to show
kindness and respect for others in the home. Children will
not know how to love when they marry unless they show
love to those with whom they live right now. But it all
begins with our love affair with the Lord. When we have
experienced the love of God, we will express it in our family

relationships—parents, brothers, sisters, husbands, wives, children, and in-laws. Ruth is ready for a beautiful love affair with Boaz because she is in love with her Lord and that love is spilling out to others in her life.

Now let us meet the Prince Charming in Ruth's future. The story implies that Boaz is much older than she (cf. Ruth 3:10). We do not know whether he was a bachelor or a widower, but we do know that he was a man of God. The Lord was an important part of his daily life. He thought often about the Lord, spoke freely of the Lord, and allowed the Lord to be a part of his everyday business dealings.

Listen to him greet his reapers in the field. "May the Lord be with you," he said. And they responded, "May the Lord bless you" (Ruth 2:4). To Ruth he declared, "May you be blessed of the Lord, my daughter" (Ruth 3:10). And again, "I will redeem you, as the Lord lives" (Ruth 3:13). All the people who attended his wedding acknowledged his dependence upon God for his future posterity: "May the Lord make the woman who is coming into your home like Rachel and Leah, both of whom built the house of Israel" (Ruth 4:11).

The first prerequisite for a successful marriage is that the man be a man of God. One reason so many marriages are floundering is because the husbands have not prepared themselves spiritually for their task. Some fellows could not think about anything but sex during their courtship days. And if it wasn't sex, it was cars or sports. They spent little or no time studying the Word, memorizing it, discovering how it applied to their lives, and learning from it what their responsibilities as Christian husbands and fathers would be. The Lord was not part of their daily living. And when they walked to the altar they were still spiritual babies, ill-prepared to assume the spiritual leadership of their homes. It is no surprise that their marriages are in trouble.

Men, if you have wasted the years until now, there is no time to lose. Start cultivating a personal walk with Jesus Christ. Spend time regularly studying the Scriptures and learning from them how God wants you to live your life and discharge your responsibilities. Begin consulting him about everything. If you are involved in an unhappy marital situation, the damage can be repaired, but the place to begin is with this matter of daily involvement with the person of Jesus Christ. Other efforts will fail until our hearts are right with him and we are growing in his likeness.

Ruth and Boaz were both ready. So we turn from their spiritual preparation to *their sterling courtship*. Naomi and Ruth had now arrived in Bethlehem, and the problem facing them was how to find enough food to eat. God had made a gracious provision in the Mosaic Law for folks in their predicament. Farmers were not permitted to reap the corners of their grain fields nor gather the gleanings; they were to leave them for the poor, for foreigners, for widows and orphans (Lev. 19:9, 10; 23:22; Deut. 24:19). Almost any way you look at it, Naomi and Ruth were qualified. They were poor widows and Ruth was a foreigner. Since Naomi was getting a little too old to work in the fields, Ruth asked if she might go and find the field of some kind man who would allow her to glean. Naomi gave her permission. "So she departed and went and gleaned in the field after the reapers; and she happened to come to the portion of the field belonging to Boaz, who was of the family of Elimelech" (Ruth 2:3).

The work was not easy—stooping and bending all day long as she gathered the grain into her long flowing cloak, the burden getting heavier with each stalk she gleaned, and the sun beating down on her back in that semi-tropical climate. A few of the bigoted hometown folks were probably taunting her because of her foreign accent, and some of the men seemed to be trying to put their hands on her (cf. Ruth 2:9). Every impulse in Ruth's body urged her to flee to the purple mountains of Moab which she could see in the distance. That was home; that was where she belonged. But with quiet courage, simple modesty, and total unselfishness, she labored on.

We fully expect Boaz to notice her. And he did. "Whose young woman is this?" he asked his servant who was in charge of the reapers. "She is the young Moabite woman who returned with Naomi from the land of Moab," he replied (Ruth 2:5, 6). Boaz lost no time in doing some nice things for Ruth. He invited her to stay in his fields and glean as much as she wanted, and to drink freely from the water pitchers provided for his own workers.

Nowhere does it say that Ruth was a beautiful woman like Sarah, Rebekah, or Rachel. We do not know whether she was or not, but we do know that she had an inner beauty, a meek and quiet spirit, an unpretentious humility that made her one of the loveliest women in Scripture. She bowed low before Boaz in genuine gratitude and said, "Why have I found favor in your sight that you should take notice of me, since I am a foreigner?" (Ruth 2:10). Her humility was evident again when she said, "You have comforted me and indeed have spoken kindly to your maidservant, though I am not like one of your maidservants" (Ruth 2:13). There was nothing put on about this. It was real. And this genuine humility, this meek and quiet spirit is one of the most valuable assets a woman can have. Peter says it is of great value in God's sight (1 Pet. 3:4). It might be a good trait for Christian women to ask God to help them develop.

It looks as though Boaz is getting more interested in this lovely woman as the day goes on. At mealtime he invited her to join him and his reapers for lunch, and he made sure she was served all that she wanted. When she finished eating and got up to return to work, Boaz said to his servants, "Let her glean even among the sheaves, and do not insult her. And also you shall purposely pull out for her some grain from the bundles and leave it that she may glean, and do not rebuke her" (Ruth 2:15, 16).

So Ruth continued to glean until evening. And when she beat out what she had gleaned, it was nearly a bushel of barley. It seems as though Boaz was a kind man, thoughtful, considerate, and gentle. There are not too many of them around anymore, judging from what many women are sharing with marriage counselors. Some men have the strange notion that kindness and gentleness are effeminate traits and they go out of their way to avoid them. Not at all! They are Christlike traits. And Christ was a rugged man's man. Surveys show that kindness and gentleness rank near the top of the characteristics women are looking for in a husband. They would be good traits for Christian men to ask God to help them develop.

Well, it was time to make a move. And strangely enough, in that culture it was Ruth's move. You see, God gave another interesting law to the Jews that required a man to marry the childless widow of his dead brother. The first son born of that union would bear his brother's name and inherit his brother's property (Deut. 25:5-10; Lev. 25:23-28). It was called the law of the "levirate" marriage, from the Hebrew word for "brother." If no brother was available, a more distant relative might be asked to fulfill this duty. But the widow would have to let him know that he was acceptable to be her "goel," as they called it, her kinsman-redeemer and provider.

Naomi told Ruth exactly how to do that. Ruth listened carefully and carried out her instructions precisely. Boaz would be sleeping on the threshing floor that night to protect his grain from thieves. After he went to sleep, Ruth tiptoed in, uncovered his feet, and laid down. By this act she was requesting Boaz to become her goel. Needless to say, Boaz was somewhat startled when he rolled over in the middle of the night and realized there was a woman lying at his feet. "Who are you?" he asked. She answered, "I am Ruth your maid. So spread your covering over your maid, for you are a close relative" (Ruth 3:9). Spreading his cloak over her would signify his willingness to become her protector and provider. His response was immediate: "May you be blessed of the Lord, my daughter. You have shown your last kindness to be better than the first by not going after young men, whether poor or rich. And now, my daughter, do not fear. I will do for you whatever you ask, for all my people in the city know that you are a woman of excellence" (Ruth 3:10, 11).

It is important to understand that there was nothing immoral in this episode. This procedure was the custom of the day, and the record emphasizes the purity of it. In the secluded darkness of the threshing room, Boaz could have gratified his human desires and no one but Ruth would have known. But he was a godly, moral, self-disciplined, Spirit-controlled man, and he kept his hands off. Scripture says that Ruth slept at his feet until morning (Ruth 3:14). Furthermore, Ruth had the reputation of being a woman of excellence (Ruth 3:11). She had physical drives like any other normal woman, but she learned to claim God's grace and strength to hold those drives in check until marriage. Boaz and Ruth both knew that God's greatest blessing in marriage would require purity before marriage. Carelessness in this area would bring guilt, loss of self-respect, and suspicion. And it could leave scars on their souls that would make their adjustment to each other in marriage most difficult.

Theirs is a vanishing viewpoint. Satan has brainwashed our society into believing premarital sex is perfectly acceptable. Most young people have experienced it before graduating from high school, and it is the rare engaged couple that even tries to refrain anymore. "But we love each other," they protest. No they don't. They love only themselves. They love to gratify their own sensual desires. If they loved each other, they would not subject each other to the hazards of disobeying God, for he says he is the avenger of all who ignore this standard (1 Thess. 4:6). It is not that God is a mean old judge who just wants to keep us from having fun. He simply knows that premarital purity will be best for us and for our marriages. Our society is paying the price for promiscuity by unprecedented marital turmoil and innumerable broken homes with all the emotional trauma they bring. God's way is always best!

Boaz and Ruth did it God's way. We are not surprised to see, finally, *their successful marriage*. Not a great deal is actually said about their relationship with each other after the wedding, but we may assume from what we have already learned about them that their marriage was richly blessed of God. Scripture does say, "So Boaz took Ruth, and she became his wife, and he went in to her. And the Lord enabled her to conceive, and she gave birth to a son" (Ruth 4:13).

The most unusual aspect of this story is the continuing role Naomi played in their lives from this point on. As a former mother-in-law, we would expect her to drop out of the picture, but Boaz and Ruth are too loving and caring to let that happen. When their baby was born, the women of Bethlehem said to Naomi, "Blessed is the Lord who has not left you without a redeemer today, and may his name become famous in Israel. May he also be to you a restorer of life and a sustainer of your old age; for your daughter-in-law, who loves you and is better to you than seven sons, has given birth to him" (Ruth 4:14, 15). Then Naomi took the baby and cared for him, and the neighbor women said, "A son has been born to Naomi!" (Ruth 4:17). Imagine that! They all considered that baby to be Naomi's own child, and Boaz and Ruth happily permitted it. Boaz continued to provide for Naomi until her death, and he seems to have done it cheerfully. And Ruth's love for her never waned. The women called Ruth "your daughter-in-law, who loves you and is better to you than seven sons."

Now that Ruth had her husband, she could have resented her former mother-in-law as an intruder. Many women would have. But when a person is filled with the love of God, his heart is big enough to engulf more than just one special person, or even a special few. He tenderly and unselfishly reaches out to meet the needs of others as well. It is striking to observe how God's love in Ruth's life overcame all obstacles—poverty, racial prejudice, age disparity, physical temptations, and even mother-in-law differences. There is a good possibility that God's love can solve the problems in our lives. As we come to understand and enjoy his unconditional love for us, and allow that love to flow through us, we think less and less about ourselves and more and more about others. And the problem-solving potential of that self-sacrificing, self-giving love is phenomenal.

Let's talk it over

1. Discuss your family backgrounds and the love shown in your homes as you were growing up.

2. Are you making your home a training ground for lessons in love? What can you do to train your children to live lovingly with others?

3. What spiritual preparation did you bring to your marriage? What can you do now to strengthen that area of your life?

4. For wives: Do you feel that you have a meek and quiet spirit? What can you do to help cultivate it?

5. For husbands: Are you kind and gentle toward your wife? How can you strengthen these traits?

6. How can God's love help you solve the problems in your life? In what ways can that love help you meet life's demands with a gracious spirit?

7. How would you describe your attitude toward your in-laws? In what ways could you give of yourself more sacrificially to improve your relationship with them?

CAUGHT IN THE
TEMPTER'S TRAP
The Story of David and Bathsheba

IF THE BIBLE were a human book, written to
magnify man, the story we are about to study
would have been carefully edited or
completely eliminated. But the Bible is a
divine book, written to glorify God, and as
surprising as the fact may be to some, this
story exalts the Lord. That is why we cannot
overlook it in our study of marriage
relationships in the Bible.

The story concerns David, the greatest hero
of Hebrew history, and by God's testimony, a
man after his own heart (1 Sam. 13:14; Acts
13:22). But men have weaknesses, even men
after God's own heart. And God is not
ashamed to share with us the weaknesses of
his greatest saints. We learn some
indispensable lessons from their mistakes,
such as the utter vileness of our hearts, the
horrible consequences of our sin, and the

unfathomable depths of God's forgiving grace. So let us learn from David.

David first gained national prominence as a teen-ager. When a teen-aged boy kills a giant of a man who has every brave Israelite soldier cowering in fear, people are going to notice. Women all over Israel were singing his praises: "Saul has slain his thousands, and David his ten thousands" (1 Sam. 18:7). In addition to that, the Bible indicates that he was extremely good looking, an extraordinary athlete, an accomplished musician, and a brilliant poet. And word had it that he would be the next king of Israel (1 Sam. 16:13). Talk about teen-age matinee idols—I would imagine every teen-aged girl in Israel had a crush on David. In fact, Scripture says, "All Israel and Judah loved David" (1 Sam. 18:16).

And who should land him but Saul's daughter, Michal. She had the inside track all along. After all, she was the king's daughter, and David was spending a lot of time around the palace. And besides that, Michal had let it be known that she was in love with David (1 Sam. 18:20). But Scripture implies that David married her more on a dare than out of genuine love. On one occasion after their marriage, Michal helped David escape from the wrath of her father (1 Sam. 19:11-17). She obviously could not go along with him under those distressing circumstances, so Saul took advantage of the situation and gave her to another man (1 Sam. 25:44). David's teen-age marriage ended in failure. Too many do. Getting married before we are fully ready to assume the responsibilities of adult life has too high a risk factor to make good sense. There is never any harm in waiting awhile to be sure.

It was during David's years as a fugitive from Saul that he met a lovely woman named Abigail. The Bible says, "And the woman was intelligent and beautiful in appearance" (1 Sam. 25:3). Her wisdom, maturity, beauty, and gracious charm completely disarmed David, and when God removed her ignorant and uncouth husband, Nabal, David lost no time in proposing marriage (1 Sam. 25:39). It was a good choice. And now that Michal was another man's wife through no fault of his, many would feel that it was acceptable to the Lord.

But the next thing we read in Scripture was clearly not acceptable. "David had also taken Ahinoam of Jezreel, and they both became his wives" (1 Sam. 25:43). David knew God had chosen him to be the next king over Israel, and he also knew what God had said about Israel's kings. Before the people ever entered the land, God warned them that someday they would want a king like the nations around them. He would allow them to appoint one of their countrymen whom he would choose, but he had to be careful not to multiply wives for himself lest they turn his heart away from the Lord (Deut. 17:14-17). Yet we learn very soon in the biblical record that David took four more wives: Maacah, Haggith, Abital, and Eglah (2 Sam. 3:2-5) And we can hardly believe our eyes when shortly after that we read, "Meanwhile David took more concubines and wives from Jerusalem" (2 Sam. 5:13).

It was not that David's physical desires were so very different from any other normal man's; it's just that most other oriental kings had harems to display their wealth and power, and David let the philosophy of the world supersede the revealed will of God. But it does reaffirm for us that David was very, very human, and it does expose to us one of his major areas of weakness.

He was somewhere in his forties now, the vulnerable age, they tell us. He had accomplished some remarkable military feats, extending the borders of Israel and securing them against every major surrounding nation. He owed himself a rest, or so he thought, and that is where our story begins. Look first at *the hollow pleasures of sin*. "Then it happened in the spring, at the time when kings go out to battle, that David sent Joab and his servants with him and all Israel, and they destroyed the sons of Ammon and besieged Rabbah. But David stayed at Jerusalem" (2 Sam. 11:1).

Kings went out to battle in spring because the winter months curtailed the movement of troops. This Ammonite campaign was a mop-up affair, left over from the previous fighting season. Israel had already defeated the Syrians whom the Ammonites had hired against them, so David probably figured that finishing the job with the Ammonites themselves would be a pushover. While his proper place was providing leadership for his men on the field of battle, he let spring fever get the best of him and he stayed at home, shirking his duty. After all, he was the king. He could do anything he pleased.

Evading responsibility is often the first step to spiritual decline. I sense a growing feeling, particularly among young people, that we can do pretty much whatever we want to do. And we don't *have* to do anything we don't want to do. This is the era of doing your own thing. It is true that we can do whatever we please, but not without paying the price spiritually. God has a plan for our lives. He has laid certain responsibilities upon us, and when we avoid them with excuses or rationalizations, we open a Pandora's box of assorted temptations that weaken our will to walk with God.

That seems to be right where David is when this scene opens. "Now when evening came David arose from his bed and walked around on the roof of the king's house" (2 Sam. 11:2). Do you get the picture? It was evening, and David was just getting out of bed. If we had any doubt about why he stayed home, it is all gone now. And it was not to catch up on his paper work. David was goofing off! "And from the roof he saw a woman bathing; and the woman was very beautiful in appearance" (2 Sam. 11:2). If he had used his head, he would have gotten off of that rooftop patio pronto. But he lingered, and let his eyes feast on every inch of Bathsheba's fleshly charms, until he could think of nothing but having her for himself.

Being tempted is no sin. But lingering over it, toying with it, flirting with it—that is inexcusable, as we saw in the case of Eve. We can tantalize ourselves to such a degree that resisting the sin is no longer considered to be a possible option. The only question that remains is *how* we are going

to do it. God says we should *flee* temptation (2 Tim. 2:22).
And he will help us handle it if we obey. But if we dawdle
and dally over it, we are doomed. When a man finds
himself attracted to a woman, for example, and either one
of them is married, he needs to get himself out of that
situation quickly. The longer he nurtures the relationship,
the harder it will be to break it off, until ultimately he will
hear himself saying stupid things like, "But I just can't
live without her." And before he realizes the implications of
what he is saying, his life and family will be in shambles.

Bathsheba is not guiltless either. She may not have
purposely enticed David, but she was immodest and
indiscreet. To disrobe and bathe in an open courtyard in full
view of any number of rooftop patios in the neighborhood
was asking for trouble. She could easily have bathed
indoors. Even so in our day, some women do not seem to
realize what the sight of their flesh can do to a man. They
allow themselves to be pushed into the fashion mold of the
world and wear revealing clothes, or nearly nothing;
then they wonder why the men they meet cannot think of
anything but sex. We must not fail to instruct our younger
girls in these matters, particularly as they enter their teen
years. Christian parents should teach their daughters
facts about the nature of man and the meaning of modesty,
then agree on standards for their dress.

David found out who the beautiful bather was, sent for
her, and the thought became the deed. There is no evidence
that this was a forcible rape. Bathsheba seems to have
been a willing partner. Her husband was off to war and she
was lonely. The glamour of being desired by the attractive
king meant more to her than her commitment to her
husband and her dedication to God. They probably
cherished those moments together; maybe they even
assured themselves that it was a tender and beautiful
experience. Most do! But in God's sight, it was hideous and
ugly. Satan had baited his trap and they were now in his
clutches.

The inevitable happened, and Bathsheba sent word to

David that she was pregnant. This was a crisis in that culture, for it would have meant death by stoning according to the Law of Moses (cf. Lev. 20:10). No crisis had ever shaken David before, and he was certainly not going to let this one destroy him. His plan was to bring Bathsheba's husband home from the battle for a few days; then nobody would ever know whose child she was carrying. But Uriah was too patriotic to enjoy his wife while his countrymen were endangering their lives on the battlefield, so he slept in the barracks with the king's servants. Then David had to put Plan B into operation. He calmly wrote Uriah's death warrant, sealed it, and sent it to Captain Joab on the front lines, delivered by Uriah's own hand. It ordered Joab to put Uriah in the fiercest part of the battle, then retreat from him. And David added murder to his adultery. After a short period of mourning, Bathsheba entered David's house and became his wife, and the two lovers finally had each other to enjoy freely and uninterruptedly . . . except for one thing: "But the thing that David had done was evil in the sight of the Lord" (2 Sam. 11:27).

That brings us to another point: *the heavy hand of discipline.* David knew he had sinned. We usually do, deep down inside. But he tried to ignore it, tried to go on living as though nothing had happened. If his conscience got too heavy, he could always rationalize by saying things like, "I'm the king, I can do as I please. It was really Bathsheba's fault, anyway. Besides, who am I hurting? Some men have to die in battle, why not Uriah?" The possibilities available to help us excuse our sin are endless. But there was something gnawing at David in the pit of his stomach, an emptiness he could not describe, accompanied by periods of extreme depression.

He later wrote three psalms describing those months out of fellowship with God: Psalms 32, 38 and 51. Listen to his plaintive cry: "I am bent over and greatly bowed down; I go mourning all day long. . . . I am benumbed and badly crushed; I groan because of the agitation of my heart" (Psa. 38:6, 8). David loved his Lord and tried to worship him, but he found a barrier there; it was the barrier of his own sin. God seemed far away. "Do not forsake me, O Lord; O my God, do not be far from me!" (Psa. 38:21). His friends sensed his irritability and avoided him. "My loved ones and my friends stand aloof from my plague; and my kinsmen stand afar off" (Psa. 38:11). David lived that way for nearly a year. He had his precious Bathsheba, but he had no rest of soul.

Then one day God sent the prophet Nathan to David with a very interesting story. "There were two men in one city, the one rich and the other poor. The rich man had a great many flocks and herds. But the poor man had nothing except one little ewe lamb which he bought and nourished; and it grew up together with him and his children. It would eat of his bread and drink of his cup and lie in his bosom, and was like a daughter to him. Now a traveler came to the rich man, and he was unwilling to take from his own flock or his own herd, to prepare for the wayfarer who had come to him; rather he took the poor man's ewe lamb and prepared it for the man who had come to him" (2 Sam. 12:1-4). When David heard the story he was furious at the rich man's selfish insensitivity and insisted that he deserved to die.

Guilt does that to us. We usually lash out most harshly and severely at the sins of others when we have the most to hide ourselves. Our subconscious anger with ourselves erupts against them.

It was with fear and trembling that Nathan uttered his next words. Other men had lost their heads for saying less than this to kings, but he was bound by his calling to deliver the message of God to the erring king. He pointed his convicting finger at David and said, "You are the man!" Then he delivered God's personal message to David: "It is I who anointed you king over Israel and it is I who delivered you from the hand of Saul. I also gave you your master's house, and your master's wives into your care, and I gave you the house of Israel and Judah; and if that had been too little, I would have added to you many more things like these! Why have you despised the word of the Lord by doing evil in His sight? You have struck down Uriah the Hittite with the sword, have taken his wife to be your wife, and have killed him with the sword of the sons of Ammon" (2 Sam. 12:7-9). And the conviction of God's Spirit penetrated the depths of David's soul.

Sin usually brings unhappy consequences, and God does not always see fit to eliminate them. He knows that experiencing the effects of our sin will help us become more sensitive to his will. The consequences of David's sin would be far-reaching and long-lasting. First, the sword would never depart from his house (2 Sam. 12:10). The people in the palace knew what was going on. They could count the months, and they realized that Uriah was not at home when the baby was conceived. It had to be David's child. Then they thought about Uriah's death, and the whole thing was much too coincidental. David's son Absalom knew it. And when he killed his half-brother Amnon for raping his sister (2 Sam. 13:28), he probably justified his actions by thinking, "Dad did it. Why can't I?" Captain Joab knew it. He was the one who carried out David's sinister command concerning Uriah. And he probably used it to excuse himself when he murdered Absalom (2 Sam. 18:14), and later Absalom's captain, Amasa (2 Sam. 20:9, 10). The sword never did depart from David's house. Our sin affects those closest to us most of all.

The second consequence of David's sin was that the Lord would raise up evil against him out of his own house (2 Sam. 12:11). Read the story of David's life and see the fulfillment of this promise for yourself: Amnon's rape of Tamar, Absalom's murder of Amnon, Absalom's rebellion against David, Adonijah's attempt to seize the throne when David was old. There was certainly evil in David's house.

Third, David's wives would be taken before his eyes and given to someone else who would lie with them in broad daylight (2 Sam. 12:11). David took another man's wife secretly; now his own wives would be taken publicly.

David and Bathsheba

During Absalom's rebellion, his followers pitched a tent on the palace roof, and Absalom had relations with his father's concubines in the sight of all Israel, fulfilling this prediction (2 Sam. 16:22).

Fourth, the child born of David's illicit union with Bathsheba would die (2 Sam. 12:14). That baby would give the enemies of God cause to blaspheme, so God graciously took the child home to himself. We grieve with David for the loss of his son, but we are grateful for this assurance of what happens to babies when they die. David says he will go to be with the child, assuring us that babies enter the presence of God (2 Sam. 12:23).

Did you notice why God took the baby, however? That point needs to be reemphasized. It was because by David's deed he had "given occasion to the enemies of the Lord to blaspheme." Now we understand one important reason for divine discipline. It is administered so the enemies of God will know that he is infinitely holy and righteous, that he will deal with sin even in his children. Were he to wink at it with a "Boys will be boys" attitude, he would become the laughingstock of the unbelieving world. David had to bear the consequences of his sin, and so must we. That burden can be heavy, but the time to think about that is before we yield.

That brings us finally to *the happy certainty of forgiveness*. Nathan's penetrating exposure of David's sin and his powerful exposition of God's righteousness brings David to his knees, acknowledging his sin: "I have sinned against the Lord," he cried (2 Sam. 12:13). These were the words God wanted to hear. David's spirit was broken; his heart was contrite (cf. Psa. 51:17). And as a result, he heard the sweetest, most beautiful, most reassuring and encouraging words known to man: "The Lord also has taken away your sin" (2 Sam. 12:13). As David put it in the Psalms, "I acknowledged my sin to Thee, and my iniquity I did not hide; I said, 'I will confess my transgressions to the Lord'; and thou didst forgive the guilt of my sin" (Psa. 32:5).

Scripture does not tell us, but I am confident that Bathsheba acknowledged her sin also and God forgave them both. While they could not erase the consequences, they could live in the full assurance of God's complete forgiveness. It was a great blot on David's life, the only major blot (cf. 1 Kgs. 15:5). But neither he nor Bathsheba let it ruin the rest of their lives. God forgave them, they forgave themselves, and they went on to live productive lives that glorified the Lord. That is exactly what God wants us to do. He does not want us to torture ourselves with the guilt of our sin. He wants us to confess it, forsake it, and forget it.

Bathsheba seems to have assumed the most prominent place among David's wives. There is no record that he ever took another wife after her. As an indication of God's forgiveness, he gave them another son whom they named Solomon, which means "peace." The Prophet Nathan called him Jedidiah, which means "Beloved of the Lord." And God assured David that Solomon, son of Bathsheba, would reign in his place and build the Temple (1 Chron. 22:9, 10). As added evidence of God's grace, Bathsheba was chosen to be one of the four women referred to in the genealogy of our Lord Jesus Christ (Matt. 1:6).

The hymn writer put it like this: "Who is a pardoning God like Thee? Or who has grace so rich and free?" That great God of grace stands ready to pardon you. Listen to the Prophet Isaiah: "Seek the Lord while He may be found; call upon Him while He is near. Let the wicked forsake his way, and the unrighteous man his thoughts; and let him return to the Lord, and He will have compassion on him; and to our God, for He will abundantly pardon" (Isa. 55:6, 7). Listen to the Apostle John: "If we confess our sins, He is faithful and righteous to forgive us our sins and to cleanse us from all unrighteousness" (1 John 1:9). It matters not how grievous your sin may have been. God stands ready to blot it out. Acknowledge it to him, then accept his gracious forgiveness.

Let's talk it over

1. Why do you think David is called a man after God's own heart in view of his dreadful sin?

2. What areas of responsibility might you be avoiding that could have a spiritually detrimental effect in the future?

3. How can you help each other avoid temptations relating to the opposite sex?

4. For wives: Is your dress consistent with God's standards or do you merely dress as the world dictates?

5. What is the meaning of modesty? How should you apply it to your life? As parents, how can you teach your daughters proper standards of dress?

6. Can you think of times when you have been especially irritable with each other because of your own burden of guilt? Honestly acknowledge those occasions to each other.

7. Did some of your own past sins come to your mind as you read this chapter, sins that you have been trying to ignore? Why not confess them to God, claim the forgiveness he promised in 1 John 1:9, then put them out of your mind once and for all?

7

MY
WAY
*The Story of
Ahab and Jezebel*

KING DAVID had been absent from the scene
of Hebrew history for about 135 years when
this story opens. His great kingdom, enlarged
and more richly endowed by his son
Solomon, had been fractured into two
weakened fragments. The southern kingdom
of Judah was being ruled by his descendants,
while the northern kingdom of Israel suffered
under a succession of wicked men at the helm.
One of them was the husband in the next
marital relationship we want to study.

He is introduced to the pages of Scripture
with these shocking words: "And Ahab the
son of Omri did evil in the sight of the Lord
more than all who were before him" (1 Kgs.
16:30). He had the dubious distinction of being
the most wicked king who reigned over
Israel up until his day. We expect almost
anything from a man that degenerate, and are

not surprised to read, "And it came about, as though it had been a trivial thing for him to walk in the sins of Jeroboam the son of Nebat, that he married Jezebel the daughter of Ethbaal king of the Sidonians, and went to serve Baal and worshiped him" (1 Kgs. 16:31).

"Sidonians" was another name for the Phoenicians, that seafaring people on the Mediterranean coast who occupied the great cities of Tyre and Sidon. With the ever-present menace of Syria and the growing threat of Assyria, Ahab decided that he needed an alliance with this neighboring nation, so he made a treaty with the king of Phoenicia and sealed it by marrying his daughter. That is how Jezebel happened to move to Samaria, the capital of Israel, and there is only one way to describe it—*a whirlwind hit Israel.*

The king of Phoenicia was not only the political leader of his people, he was also the high priest of their religion, as his name Ethbaal implies. Jezebel had grown up steeped in the worship of Baal and his female consort, Astarte (or Ashtoreth). Baal was considered to be the god of the *land.* He owned it, they said, and he controlled its weather and the increase of its crops and cattle. Ashtoreth was considered to be the mother-goddess of fertility. So idols of both Baal and Ashtoreth stood side by side in their temples and were worshiped by priests and temple prostitutes with lewd dances and sacred orgies, with the hope that their god and goddess would follow their example and increase the productivity of their agriculture, their animals, and their children. In times of crisis such as famine, they slashed themselves and even sacrificed their children to appease the gods and implore their help.

Jezebel was fanatical about her religion. The worship of Jehovah must have seemed dull and commonplace by comparison, and she was determined to change it. She was a headstrong, self-willed, domineering woman, and with a moral weakling for a husband, she had little trouble getting her way. She got him to build a house for Baal beside the palace in Samaria, as well as an "Ashtoreth," that is, an idol of the fertility goddess. Then she brought 450 prophets of Baal and 400 prophets of Ashtoreth from Phoenicia, housed them in the palace, and fed them in royal style. Their duties would have been to promote the worship of Baal and Ashtoreth throughout the land.

Not satisfied to establish her religion in Israel, Jezebel sought to stamp out every remnant of Jehovah worship and to kill every true prophet of God. She had to have things completely her way, and she almost succeeded. Some prophets survived by compromising their convictions and turning into "yes" men for Ahab. Another group of 100 were hidden in a cave and fed secretly by a godly servant of Ahab named Obadiah. But Elijah was the only one courageous enough to stand up openly against Jezebel's wickedness. God gave him a great victory when he called down fire from heaven upon Mount Carmel. The prophets of Baal were slain and it looked as though the nation would turn back to God. But Jezebel was not finished with her sinister work. She swore in her rage that she would kill Elijah, and he ran for his life, collapsed in the wilderness under a juniper tree, and pleaded with God to let him die. It was the lowest point in the godly prophet's great career. And Baal worship lived on, dragging the nation to new depths of degradation. This stubborn, headstrong, self-willed wife of Ahab brought disruption and distress to Israel for years to come.

Marriages to stubborn, willful people can bring unhappiness to all concerned. Their indomitable self-will which has never been surrendered to God will seldom give in to those around them. With unyielding obstinacy they keep demanding their own way and looking for every possible means and method of doing or having what they want. They will not listen to reason; they will not consider the feelings of others; they will not face the potential consequences of their intended actions. They believe that they are right and others are wrong, and they are determined to have everything their way. They obviously know very little of God's love which "does not seek its own" (1 Cor. 13:5), but have only self-love which insists on its own rights and demands its own way. Those who live with people like this eventually find themselves emotionally destroyed. For the survival of those around us, for the happiness of our mates and for harmony in our marriages, we must face up to every trace of stubborn self-will and claim God's grace to deal with it.

Of course, Ahab was just as self-willed as Jezebel, but with a different temperament. For one thing, he had willfully entered a marriage that was politically convenient, but contrary to every word from God. But Ahab's self-will becomes even more evident in an incident involving *the king and his vegetable garden*. Shortly after his marriage to Jezebel, Ahab not only beautified the palace at Samaria so that it came to be called "the ivory house" (1 Kgs. 22:39), but he also built a second palace in Jezreel, twenty-five miles to the north, in an area of a more moderate climate in the wintertime. "Now is came about after these things, that Naboth the Jezreelite had a vineyard which was in Jezreel beside the palace of Ahab king of Samaria" (1 Kgs. 21:1). Ahab decided he wanted Naboth's property, so he went to him and said, "Give me your vineyard, that I may have it for a vegetable garden because it is close beside my house, and I will give you a better vineyard than it in its place; if you like, I will give you the price of it in money" (1 Kgs. 21:2). Naboth declined the offer, just as he should have done, for God had forbidden the Jews to sell their paternal inheritance (Lev. 25:23-34). Naboth was simply obeying the law of the Lord.

"So Ahab came into his house sullen and vexed because of the word which Naboth the Jezreelite had spoken to him . . . . And he lay down on his bed and turned away his face and ate no food" (1 Kgs. 21:4). Can you believe that a grown man would act this childishly? Some do. Weak, vacillating people like Ahab often want their own way just as much as headstrong, domineering people like Jezebel. But they react differently when they do not get it. While the forceful ones rant and rave, strike out at those who stand in their way, throw fits and destroy things, the weak ones

78

sulk and pout and fret like spoiled children. They may refuse to get out of bed and even refuse to eat. They just want to feel sorry for themselves and let everybody know how bad things are for them. All they really succeed in doing is letting people know how self-centered and immature they are.

Self-will of either variety, the violent kind or the peevish kind, can ruin a marriage. The trouble often starts when our mates infringe upon our inviolable rights. Maybe the husband will not let his wife buy something she thinks she has a right to have, or the wife prepares an absolutely terrible dinner on the very day hubby is expecting his favorite dish. Instead of letting the love and graciousness of Jesus Christ control us, our sinful natures take over and we go into our rage routine or sulk syndrome, whichever it is with us. And it slowly but surely eats away at our relationship. And that inflexible self-will which has never been broken and yielded to God may ultimately lead to much greater problems. I have heard some say, "I don't love her anymore. I don't want her. I'm going to find some happiness for myself and I don't care what the Bible says."

God wants to break our sinful, stubborn wills. He wants to conquer them with his love. The first step to victory is simply to admit that continually demanding our own way is disobedience to God's Word, and therefore sin. Talk to the Lord about it. Be honest with him. Tell him frankly that you would rather have your own way than be unselfish and considerate of others, but acknowledge that it is contrary to his Word. Ask him to help you. Then by an act of your will, determine to do the loving thing. That step of faith will open the channel of God's power. He will not only enable you to carry through with your decision to act in love, but he will give you genuine delight in doing his will.

But go back to Ahab and his vegetable garden for a moment. Jezebel found Ahab sulking in his bed and said to him, "How is it that your spirit is so sullen that you are not eating food?" (1 Kgs. 21:5). So he explained to her how

79

Naboth refused to let him have his vegetable garden. She replied, "Do you now reign over Israel?" (1 Kgs. 21:7). In modern terms, that might sound more like, "What are you, a man or a mouse? Squeak up! Don't you know that you are the king? You can take anything you want." With her Phoenician background, Jezebel could not seem to understand that even the king in Israel was subject to the laws of God.

We discover how thoroughly this weak and wicked man was dominated by his overbearing wife when she said, "Arise, eat bread, and let your heart be joyful; I will give you the vineyard of Naboth the Jezreelite" (1 Kgs. 21:7). She planned to commit a hideous crime; she was going to pay two false witnesses to testify that they heard Naboth blaspheme God and the king, so that both he and his sons would be stoned to death and the king would be free to lay claim to his land (cf. 2 Kgs. 9:26). She was going to teach Ahab her philosophy of life: "Take what you want and destroy anyone who stands in your way." And Ahab did not have the courage to stop her.

A man will do strange things when he is taunted and ridiculed by his wife. "Why didn't you stand up to him?" one wife jeered when she heard of her husband's latest disagreement with the boss. "When are you going to start acting like a man?" So the next time he did, and he lost his job and everyone suffered. So the next round went like this: "You can't even provide for your family. What kind of a man are you?" So he showed her by roughing her up a little, and then by turning to cheating and stealing to make ends meet. And again, everyone in the family suffered. A man needs respect from his wife, not ridicule. Of this disgraceful incident in Ahab's life, God said, "Surely there was no one like Ahab who sold himself to do evil in the sight of the Lord, because Jezebel his wife incited him" (1 Kgs. 21:25). Some men need to be spurred on, to be sure, but not to do evil! A godly wife will challenge her husband to listen to God and live for him, not encourage him to sin.

But the story is not over. These two were *self-willed to the end*. Elijah met Ahab in Naboth's vineyard and pronounced God's judgment on both him and his wife for their wicked deed. It was several years later when that judgment came on Ahab, and it too is a story of self-will. The incident started over a city east of Jordan called Ramoth-Gilead, which Ahab said belonged to Israel but was still in the hands of Syria. When Jehoshaphat, King of Judah, came to visit Ahab, he asked him if he would go to battle with him for Ramoth-Gilead. Jehoshaphat agreed, but wanted to consult the Lord first. Ahab called his "yes" men together and they assured him that the Lord would give Ramoth-Gilead into the hand of the king. But Jehoshaphat was still not satisfied. He wanted another opinion: "Is there not yet a prophet of the Lord here, that we may inquire of him?" (1 Kgs. 22:7). And Ahab replied, "There is yet one man by whom we may inquire of the Lord, but I hate him, because he does not prophesy good concerning me, but evil. He is Micaiah son of Imlah" (1 Kgs. 22:8). So Micaiah was called, and although he knew his life was in danger, he spoke what God told him. Israel would be scattered on the mountains like sheep without a shepherd (1 Kgs. 22:17). As we might expect, Ahab rejected Micaiah's prophecy and had him cast into prison. He was going to have what he wanted and do what he pleased, regardless of God's will.

But it didn't work out quite like he planned. Ahab knew the Syrians would be after him personally, so he removed his royal garments and disguised himself as a regular soldier. "Now a certain man drew his bow at random and struck the king of Israel in a joint of the armor" (1 Kgs. 22:34). That soldier did not know he was shooting at the king, but his arrow penetrated the narrow slit between the pieces of Ahab's armor. Very few bowmen would have been that accurate. It was obvious that God was guiding that arrow, and Ahab's self-will ended in his untimely death.

Jezebel outlived him by almost fourteen years. Jehu, the

captain of Israel's army, was to be the instrument of divine
discipline in her case. After slaying King Jehoram, the
son of Ahab, he rode to Jezreel. Scripture says, "When Jehu
came to Jezreel, Jezebel heard of it, and she painted
her eyes and adorned her head, and looked out the
window" (2 Kgs. 9:30). She knew what was about to
happen, but she was going to die like a queen, arrogant,
self-willed and unrepentant to the end. She shouted
abuses at Jehu from her upstairs window, but at Jehu's
command, several of her servants threw her down, "and
some of her blood was sprinkled on the wall and on the
horses, and he trampled her under foot" (2 Kgs. 9:33). It
was a violent death, but it illustrated again the seriousness
of sinful self-will in opposition to God.

Yet *their influence lived on* in their children. And this is
often the saddest side effect of lives like Ahab's and
Jezebel's. Two sons of Ahab and Jezebel later ruled in Israel.
The first was Ahaziah. Of him God says, "And he did
evil in the sight of the Lord and walked in the way of his
father and in the way of his mother and in the way of
Jeroboam the son of Nebat, who caused Israel to sin. So he
served Baal and worshiped him and provoked the Lord God
of Israel to anger according to all that his father had done"
(1 Kgs. 22:52, 53). The second son to reign was Jehoram.
As Jehu rode to execute vengeance on the house of Ahab,
Jehoram cried, "Is it peace, Jehu?" Jehu summed up
Jehoram's reign with his reply: "What peace, so long as the
harlotries of your mother Jezebel and her witchcrafts
are so many?" (2 Kgs. 9:22).

Ahab and Jezebel also had a daughter, Athaliah, and she
married another man named Jehoram, the son of
Jehoshaphat, king of the southern kingdom of Judah. "And
he walked in the way of the kings of Israel, just as the house
of Ahab did (for Ahab's daughter was his wife), and he
did evil in the sight of the Lord" (2 Chron. 21:6). So it was
that the evil influence moved south. At Jehoram's death,
his son by Athaliah became king of Judah. "Ahaziah
was twenty-two years old when he became king, and he

reigned one year in Jerusalem. And his mother's name was Athaliah, the granddaughter of Omri. He also walked in the ways of the house of Ahab, for his mother was his counselor to do wickedly. And he did evil in the sight of the Lord like the house of Ahab, for they were his counselors after the death of his father, to his destruction" (2 Chron. 22:2-4). And the evil influence lived on!

God only knows how many generations will be affected by our sinful self-will, our insistence on having things our way instead of God's. This shocking story ought to provide the incentive we need to put off every remnant of self-will and yield ourselves fully to do the will of God.

Let's talk it over

1. How do you think Ahab should have handled the situation when it became obvious to him that Jezebel wanted to eliminate Jehovah worship from Israel?

2. How can a wife increase her respect for her husband? How can a husband help her?

3. Do you feel that your mate is infringing on any of your "inviolable rights"? Discuss with each other how the situation can be handled.

4. Which way does your selfish nature exhibit itself—with rage or with sullenness? What clues help you recognize your rising self-will? What can you do to combat it?

5. Do you seem to be demanding your own way much of the time? Ask your mate what he or she thinks, then prayerfully consider the answer.

6. Have you both yielded yourselves to Christ as lord of your lives and are you willing to let him make the changes necessary to improve your relationship with each other? (Your willingness to hear your mate out without getting irritable or defensive may be an accurate measure of that willingness.)

UNDYING
LOVE
The Story of
Hosea and Gomer

THE CALENDAR on the wall indicated that it
was about 760 years before Jesus was born.
Jeroboam II was on the throne of the northern
kingdom of Israel, and his military exploits
had extended Israel's borders farther than
they had been since the days of Solomon's
glorious kingdom. Tribute money from
subject nations was pouring into the treasury
at the capital city of Samaria, and the people
of Israel were enjoying a period of
unprecedented prosperity.

As is often the case, with prosperity came
moral and spiritual degeneration. Secularism
and materialism captured the hearts of the
people and sin ran rampant. The list reads like
twentieth-century America: swearing, lying,
killing, stealing, adultery, drunkenness,
perversion, perjury, deceit, and oppression,
to name but a few. But the thing that grieved

the heart of God more than anything else was the sin of idolatry (Hos. 4:12, 13; 13:2). The golden calves set up by Jeroboam I about 150 years earlier had opened the floodgates to every evil expression of Canaanite idolatry, including drunkenness, religious prostitution and human sacrifice.

Since the Lord viewed Israel as his wife, he viewed her worship of other gods as spiritual adultery. The Old Testament speaks frequently of Israel whoring after or playing the harlot with other gods (e.g., Deut. 31:16; Judg. 2:17). Jehovah had told Israel from the beginning that he would not share her with others. "You shall have no other gods before Me" was the first of his ten great commandments (Ex. 20:3). But she had persistently ignored his command, and by the days of Jeroboam II the situation was intolerable. God was about to speak decisively and he chose first a prophet named Amos. The former herdsman of Tekoa thundered God's warning of imminent judgment, but the nation paid little attention. So God spoke again, this time through the prophet Hosea whose name meant "Jehovah is salvation."

The very first thing God ever said to Hosea tells us about *his unlikely marriage*: "Go, take to yourself a wife of harlotry, and have children of harlotry; for the land commits flagrant harlotry, forsaking the Lord" (Hos. 1:2). These instructions have been variously understood by different students of Scripture through the years. Some believe that God was commanding Hosea to marry a woman who had formerly been a prostitute. Others contend that taking a wife of harlotry would merely refer to marrying a woman from the northern kingdom of Israel, a land which was guilty of spiritual adultery. In either case, it is obvious that she was a woman who had been deeply affected by the moral laxity of her society, and God intended to use the prophet's personal relationship with her as a penetrating object lesson of his own relationship with his unfaithful people, Israel. Whatever her past, there may have been some evidence of genuine repentance and faith in Jehovah. Maybe she had responded to the Spirit-filled ministry of Hosea himself, and he found his heart drawn to her in deep and unselfish love. God directed him to take her as his wife, and so it was that Gomer, the daughter of Diblaim, became the unlikely wife of the budding young preacher.

The early days of their marriage were beautiful as their love began to blossom. And God blessed their union with a son. How Hosea's heart must have swelled with joy. He was convinced that his marriage would be better than ever with this little one to brighten their home. God named the baby, for his name was to have prophetic significance to the nation. He called him Jezreel, because it was at Jezreel that King Jeroboam's great grandfather Jehu had first come to the throne by ambitious crimes of bloodshed and violence. While his dynasty was prospering at the moment, its destruction was on the horizon and it would happen in the valley of Jezreel (Hos. 1:4, 5).

It was after the birth of Jezreel that Hosea seems to have noticed a change in Gomer. She became restless and unhappy, like a bird trapped in a cage. He went on preaching, encouraging the wayward nation to turn from its sin and trust God for deliverance from the threat of surrounding nations. "Return unto the Lord!" was the theme of his message, and he preached it repeatedly with power (Hos. 6:1; 14:1). But Gomer seemed less and less interested in his ministry. In fact, she may have grown to resent it. She probably even accused Hosea of thinking more about his preaching than he did of her. She began to find other interests to occupy herself, and spent more and more time away from home.

The dangers are great when a husband and wife have few interests in common. Sometimes he goes his way and she goes hers. They each have their own set of friends, and there is little communication to bring their two worlds together. A husband's preoccupation with his work may be the major contributing factor to the cleavage. Or it may be a wife's growing involvement in outside activities and subsequent neglect of the home. It may simply be a disinterest in the things of the Lord on the part of either husband or wife. But it sets the scene for great calamity. Husbands and wives need to do things together and take an interest in each other's activities. In this inspired story, the responsibility is clearly laid upon Gomer rather than Hosea. She did not share her husband's love for God.

That brings us, secondly, to *his unrelieved agony*. Scripture does not give us the details of what happened, but what it does say would permit us some speculation concerning the progressive trend that led to the tragic situation we eventually discover. Gomer's absences from home probably grew more frequent and prolonged and soon Hosea was feeling pangs of suspicion about her faithfulness to him. He lay awake at night and wrestled with his fears. He preached with a heavy heart during the day. And his suspicions were confirmed when Gomer got pregnant again. It was a girl this time, and Hosea was convinced that the child was not his. At God's direction, he called her Loruhamah, which means "unpitied" or "unloved," implying that she would not enjoy her true father's love. Again the name was symbolic of Israel's wandering from God's love and the discipline she would soon experience. But even that spiritual message could not soothe the prophet's troubled soul.

No sooner had little Loruhamah been weaned than Gomer conceived again. It was another boy. God told Hosea to call him Lo-ammi, which meant "not my people," or "no kin of mine." It symbolized Israel's alienation from Jehovah, but it also exposed Gomer's sinful escapades. That child born in Hosea's house was not his.

It was all out in the open now. Everyone knew about Gomer's affairs. While the entire second chapter of Hosea's prophecy describes Jehovah's relationship with his unfaithful wife Israel, it is difficult to escape the feeling that it grows out of Hosea's relationship with Gomer, sandwiched as it is between two chapters that clearly describe that sad and sordid story. He pleaded with her

(2:2). He threatened to disinherit her (2:3). But still she ran off with her lovers because they promised to lavish material things on her (2:5). He tried to stop her on occasion (2:6), but she continued to seek her companions in sin (2:7). Hosea would take her back in loving forgiveness and they would try again. But her repentance would be short-lived and soon she would be off again with another new lover.

Then the final blow fell. Maybe it was a note, maybe word sent by a friend, but the essence of it seems to have been, "I'm leaving for good this time. I've found my true love. I'll never come back again." How Hosea must have suffered! He loved her deeply and grieved for her as though she had been taken in death. His heart ached that she should choose a life that would surely bring her to ruin. His friends were probably saying, "Good riddance to her, Hosea. Now you'll be through with her adulterous ways once and for all." But Hosea did not feel that way. He longed for her to come home.

We cannot escape the message of *his undying love*. Hosea wanted to see Gomer restored to his side as his faithful wife. And he believed that God was great enough to do it. One day word came by way of the grapevine gossips that Gomer had been deserted by her lover. She had sold herself into slavery and had hit bottom. This was the last straw. Certainly now Hosea would forget her. But his heart said "No." He could not give her up. And then God spoke to him: "Go again, love a woman who is loved by her husband, yet an adulteress, even as the Lord loves the sons of Israel, though they turn to other gods" (Hos. 3:1).

Gomer was still beloved of Hosea even though she was an adulteress, and God wanted him to seek her out and prove his love to her. How could anyone love that deeply? The answer was right there in God's instructions to Hosea, "even as the Lord loves." Only one who knows the love and forgiveness of God can ever love this perfectly. And one who has experienced his loving forgiveness cannot help but love and forgive others. Christian husbands are commanded to love their wives as Christ loved the Church (Eph. 5:25), and Hosea is an outstanding biblical example of that kind of love.

So he began his search, driven by that indestructible divine love, love that bears all things, believes all things, hopes all things, endures all things, love that never ends. And he found her, ragged, torn, sick, dirty, disheveled, destitute, chained to an auction block in a filthy slave market, a repulsive shadow of the woman she once was. We wonder how anyone could love her now. But Hosea bought her from her slavery for fifteen shekels of silver and thirteen bushels of barley (Hos. 3:2). Then he said to her, "You shall stay with me for many days. You shall not play the harlot, nor shall you have a man; so I will also be toward you" (Hos. 3:3). He actually paid for her, brought her home, and eventually restored her to her position as his wife. While we do not find anything else in Scripture about their relationship with each other, we assume that God used Hosea's supreme act of forgiving love to melt her heart and change her life.

How many times should a husband or wife forgive? Some contend, "If I keep forgiving I simply affirm him in his pattern of sin." Or "If I keep forgiving, she'll think she can get away with anything she wants." Others say, "If I keep forgiving, it's like putting my seal of approval on his behavior." Or "I can't take another hurt like that. If he does that one more time, I'm leaving." Those are human responses. Listen to the response of the Lord Jesus. You see, Peter had asked the Lord this same question: "Lord, how often shall my brother sin against me and I forgive him? Up to seven times?" The Lord's answer was, "I do not say to you, up to seven times, but up to seventy times seven" (Matt. 18:21, 22). That is a great deal of forgiveness. In fact, Christ was simply saying in a captivating way that there is no end to forgiveness.

Sometimes it's just the little slights and daily agitations that need forgiveness, the occasional sharp word or angry accusation. But we harbor it, let it eat at us, and build up bitterness and resentment which erodes our relationship. Maybe it's a major offense, like Gomer's, and we can never forget it. We stew on it and fret over it, and we keep bringing it up in a subconscious attempt to punish our mates for the hurts we have suffered. We try to forgive, but a few days later it's right there again, preying on our consciousness. Big wounds sometimes take longer to heal. They will come back to our minds. There is no way to avoid it. But every time they do, we must first remind ourselves that we really did forgive, then rehearse how much God has forgiven us, then ask him to take the destructive, unforgiving thoughts out of our minds.

Forgiveness does not necessarily mean that we must suffer in silence. The need for open and honest communication would demand that we share what we think and how we feel, what the wrong has done to us, and how our mates can help us get over it. God tells us how much our sin grieves him. Gomer certainly knew how her affairs were tearing at Hosea's heart. What we say must be said lovingly and kindly, but we have both the need and the obligation to share what is on our hearts.

Neither does forgiveness necessarily mean we cannot take positive steps to guard against the sin recurring. That might require some extended counseling; it might demand an honest reappraisal of our personalities or habit patterns; it might mean a change in our life-style or a relocation. God takes positive steps to help us want to please him. That is what divine discipline is all about. We do not discipline each other, but we can discuss steps that will help us avoid these same pitfalls in the future.

Forgiveness does mean, however, that we will pay for the other person's offenses. We will refuse to retaliate in any way to make the guilty person pay. We will absolve him of all guilt. God can use that forgiving love to melt hardened hearts and change calloused lives quicker than anything else in this whole wide world. That is the lesson of Hosea and Gomer, the lesson of forgiveness. God's love and forgiveness pervade Hosea's entire prophecy. Please do not misunderstand it. God hates sin; it grieves his heart; he cannot condone it; his perfect righteousness and justice demand that he deal with it. But he still loves sinners and diligently seeks them out and offers them his loving forgiveness.

God's ancient people Israel kept going back to their sins. "What shall I do with you, O Ephraim? What shall I do with you, O Judah? For your loyalty is like a morning cloud, and like the dew which goes away early" (Hos. 6:4). But God never stopped loving them. "When Israel was a youth I loved him, and out of Egypt I called My son" (Hos. 11:1). "I led them with cords of a man, with bonds of love" (Hos. 11:4). "How can I give you up, O Ephraim? How can I surrender you, O Israel?" (Hos. 11:8). And because he never stopped loving them, he never stopped pleading with them: "Return, O Israel, to the Lord your God, for you have stumbled because of your iniquity" (Hos. 14:1).

We need to love like that. We need to forgive like that. We need to drag the festering hurts we have been harboring in our hearts to the cross of Christ—where we laid our own burden of guilt one day and where we found God's loving forgiveness—and we must leave them all there. When we fully forgive, our minds will be released from the bondage of resentment that has been building a wall between us, and we shall be free to grow in our relationship with each other.

Let's talk it over

1. What do you think are the major causes for husbands and wives drifting apart?

2. What interests do you both share in common? What else could you do together to strengthen your bond of oneness?

3. Husbands and wives are not always aware of each other's love. It might be helpful for each of you to finish the following

statements: "I feel loved when you..." "I am saying that I love you when..."

4. Can you think of wrongs you have suffered from your mate that may be keeping you from freely expressing your love? Admit them to your mate and verbalize your full forgiveness.

5. How can you keep the wrongs for which you have forgiven others from creeping back into your mind and destroying your peace?

6. What positive steps can you and your mate take to keep certain sins from repeating themselves in your lives?

FOR SUCH
A TIME AS THIS
The Story of Ahasuerus and Esther

THE SITUATIONS in our lives are not always to
our liking: the places we must live, the people
we must associate with, or the problems we
encounter. And these things may not always
be our fault. We may have been the victims of
circumstances, or we may have made
decisions which we thought were right but
which have not worked out as we expected.
Some people feel that way about their
marriages—the woman, for example, who
thought the man she married was a believer.
She later found out that he had deceived her.
His actions continually reflected his disinterest
in the things of the Lord and caused her
endless grief. There is a story in God's Word
that will encourage folks in adverse
circumstances such as these.

The man of the house was none other than
the king of the greatest empire in the world of

his day. The Jews called him Ahasuerus, the Hebrew form of his Persian name. Secular history knows him better by his Greek name, King Xerxes I who ruled Persia from 486 to 465 B.C. His powerful empire spread from India to Ethiopia (Esth. 1:1). But that wasn't enough for him. The real passion of his life was to do what his father, Darius I, had never been able to do—conquer Greece.

The Word of God tells us that "in the third year of his reign, he gave a banquet for all his princes and attendants, the army officers of Persia and Media, the nobles, and the princes of his provinces being in his presence, when he displayed the riches of his royal glory and the splendor of his great majesty for many days, 180 days" (Esth. 1:3, 4). Such a high-level conference, lasting six months, had to be more than just a big party. It was probably a strategy session for Xerxes' forthcoming invasion of Greece. Secular history tells us that he began that invasion not long after this magnificent convocation, in 481 B.C.

To conclude the conference, however, he planned seven special days of celebration and feasting (Esth. 1:5). When he was a little tipsy from his wine, he called for his beautiful queen, Vashti, so that he could show her off before his friends (Esth. 1:11). She refused to be made a public spectacle, and Ahasuerus was enraged. At the advice of his trusted counselors he decided to depose her by royal decree—the law of the Medes and the Persians which could never be reversed, not even by the king himself (Esth. 1:19). It was a rash decision which he would live to regret, but Ahasuerus was known to be an impulsive and headstrong man.

Besides that, he had more important things to do than worry about his harem. He was ready to conquer Greece. His armies were superior to theirs and the momentum of history was on his side. But in a succession of famous battles familiar to students of ancient history (Thermopylae, Salamis, Plataea), his military might was finally broken, and he returned to his capital at Susa a beaten man. How he must have longed for the comfort and companionship of his deposed queen to soothe him in his shame and put his fractured ego back together. "After these things when the anger of King Ahasuerus had subsided, he remembered Vashti and what she had done and what had been decreed against her" (Esth. 2:1). But it was too late. His decree was irreversible.

That is when his aides suggested an all-Persia beauty contest to find *a queen for King Ahasuerus*. "Let beautiful young virgins be sought for the king. And let the king appoint overseers in all the provinces of his kingdom that they may gather every beautiful young virgin to Susa the capital, to the harem, into the custody of Hegai, the king's eunuch, who was in charge of the women; and let their cosmetics be given them. Then let the young lady who pleases the king be queen in place of Vashti" (Esth. 2:2-4). The whole thing sounded like fun to the king, so he gave his permission, and the search was on. A beauty contest is not a bad way to find a wife, if good looks are all you are looking for. But our sovereign God was going to give Ahasuerus a great deal more than good looks, whether he wanted it or not. God already had a wife picked out for this heathen king. Although God's name is nowhere mentioned in this book, his providential hand is clearly visible, ruling and overruling in the affairs of men.

Unknown to Ahasuerus, the next queen of Persia was to be a young Jewess. She would probably have rather been in Jerusalem with her countrymen, but for some reason her parents had declined to go back when King Cyrus gave his permission fifty years earlier. The Jews in captivity had been allowed to settle down, open businesses, and live normal lives, and only 50,000 of them chose to return to Israel when they had the opportunity.

This woman's parents were dead and her older cousin, Mordecai, was raising her. Scripture says, "And he was bringing up Hadassah, that is Esther, his uncle's daughter, for she had neither father nor mother. Now the young lady was beautiful of form and face, and when her father and her mother died, Mordecai took her as his own

daughter" (Esth. 2:7). She was a lovely woman, and there
was no way she could escape the clutches of the king's
servants who were scouring the land for beautiful women.
"So it came about when the command and decree of the
king were heard and many young ladies were gathered to
Susa the capital into the custody of Hegai, that Esther was
taken to the king's palace into the custody of Hegai, who
was in charge of the women" (Esth. 2:8).

Mordecai checked on Esther's welfare daily, since he was
a gatekeeper at the palace. He instructed her not to
make her nationality known to anyone, probably to guard
her against the unkind treatment directed against Jews in
almost every country they have ever lived in, throughout
their history, and she dutifully obeyed. Then when it was
her turn to be ushered in to the king's presence, she
asked for nothing special with which to impress him, as the
other girls had done. Her natural God-given beauty and
evident loveliness of spirit alone captured the heart of the
king. "And the king loved Esther more than all the
women, and she found favor and kindness with him more
than all the virgins, so that he set the royal crown on her
head and made her queen instead of Vashti" (Esth. 2:17).

Scripture never says that Esther wanted to marry
Ahasuerus. It was a flattering offer, but she must have
known that he would be less than an ideal husband,
especially after what had happened to Vashti. But how do
you say "no" to a tyrannical monarch without losing
your head? So it was that this simple Jewish girl became the
queen of the Persian empire. It was a rags to riches story
unexcelled in human history.

The chronology of the book indicates that it was about
five years later when the bubble burst and we find *a crisis
for God's people*. The culprit who caused the trouble must
have been Hitler's Old Testament hero. He was a vicious,
anti-Semitic Amalakite named Haman, evidently a
descendant of Agag, king of the Amalakites, whom King
Saul had kept alive in disobedience to the command of the
Lord (1 Sam. 15:8, 9). When Ahasuerus made him prime

minister, everybody in the palace bowed down to him
except Mordecai. He would bow his knee to none but God,
and that infuriated Haman. He vowed not only to punish
Mordecai, but to exterminate every living Jew in the
Persian empire, and incidentally, that would include those
in the land of Israel as well, for they were part of the
empire. Haman got the king to agree to his plan and it was
sealed with the king's ring, the irreversible law of the
Medes and the Persians. It was another hasty decision that
Ahasuerus would live to regret.

"When Mordecai learned all that had been done, he tore
his clothes, put on sackcloth and ashes, and went out
into the midst of the city and wailed loudly and bitterly.
And he went as far as the king's gate, for no one was
to enter the king's gate clothed in sackcloth. And in each
and every province where the command and decree of the
king came, there was great mourning among the Jews, with
fasting, weeping, and wailing; and many lay on sackcloth
and ashes" (Esth. 4:1-3).

Strange as it may seem, prayer is never specifically
mentioned in this book, just as the name of God is never
mentioned, but you can be sure that these Jews were
praying. Fasting is referred to, and that is usually
associated with prayer in Scripture. And the wailing
probably indicates a desperate cry to God. These Jews were
away from their land by their own choice, out of the place
of blessing, separated from their place of worship, and
that may be why neither God nor prayer are directly
mentioned. But they were praying, and God was watching
over them, superintending their circumstances to glorify his
own name. He is doing the same for us even when we are
not aware of it.

We are about to discover that there is *a purpose for God's
appointments*. This revelation is made through an exchange
of communications between Esther and Mordecai. Esther
sent one of the king's chamberlains to find out why
Mordecai was in mourning. Mordecai sent a message back
explaining the whole diabolical plot, of which she was

unaware, and encouraging her to intercede with the king. She answered quickly, reminding him that no one entered the king's presence without being invited unless he was tired of living, and that the king had not invited her into his presence for a full month. There was one slim possibility—if the king saw her and extended his golden scepter, she could enter.

Mordecai may have missed God's best by not returning to Israel, but his spiritual insight had increased since then. He was beginning to understand something of God's sovereign grace and divine providence, beginning to see that God can use even the adversities of life to accomplish his purposes. He sent word back to Esther, "Do not imagine that you in the king's palace can escape any more than all the Jews. For if you remain silent at this time, relief and deliverance will arise for the Jews from another place and you and your father's house will perish. And who knows whether you have not attained royalty for such a time as this?" (Esth. 4:13, 14). Esther is really no safer than any other Jew. When it becomes known that she is Jewish, her life will be endangered too. Mordecai is convinced that God is going to care for his people Israel, however. They may be far from him, but he cannot let them perish, for that would be contrary to his promises. If he does not use Esther to deliver them, he will use some other means. He is a sovereign God.

You see, Mordecai had grasped the fact that God allowed them to remain in Persia, and may now be ready to turn their decision to stay into glory for himself and deliverance for the Jewish people. "And who knows whether you have not attained royalty for such a time as this." What an outstanding illustration of the greatness of our God. He can take not only the circumstances of our lives that are beyond our control, but he can take the wrong decisions we have made, and even the sins we have committed, and work them out for good. The psalmist says: "For the wrath of man shall praise Thee" (Psa. 76:10). If God can make man's wrath praise him, he can certainly make our sins and shortcomings praise him.

That obviously does not mean we should live our lives in total disregard for the will of God, and then expect him to work out the mess we make. There is an enormous load of unhappiness and sorrow on that road, as many Christians will testify. The consequences of willful sin can be unbearable. It does mean that when we put our lives in Christ's hands and yield ourselves unreservedly to him, we can be certain that he has a great plan for us from that moment on. He can use everything that has happened to us in the past and every circumstance in our present experience to help carry out that plan.

God has a purpose for you, right now, right where you are, no matter who you are, where you live, to whom you are married, what you have experienced in the past, or what you are facing in the future. In fact he has allowed you to come to this place in your life for a definite purpose, "for such a time as this." He has something specific for you to accomplish in your present situation, and he wants you to look for the opportunities in that present sphere of influence.

You see, believers are a part of God's great program on earth; they should be living with confidence as people of destiny. God does not want us moaning over our plight and looking for a way out. He will be honored when we claim his grace to be what he wants us to be and do what he wants us to do in our present circumstances. We must take advantage of the opportunities he has made available to us in the here and now. He may later open wider spheres of opportunity if that suits his purposes, but that is in his hands. Our responsibility is to let him use us where we are.

Esther responded positively to Mordecai's godly advice. She sent word saying, "Go, assemble all the Jews who are found in Susa, and fast for me; do not eat or drink for three days, night or day. I and my maidens also will fast in the same way. And thus I will go in to the king, which is not acording to the law; and if I perish, I perish" (Esth. 4:16). Her reference to fasting would reveal her great confidence in the power of prayer, particularly in the fellowship of other believers in prayer. If we are facing trying circumstances, it might be wise to solicit the prayer support of other Christians. We do not need to air all our dirty linen, run down our spouses or gossip about anybody else involved in the problem. All we need to do is admit that we have a need and ask our friends to stand with us in prayer.

With that shroud of prayer surrounding and protecting us, the next step is to determine in our hearts that we shall do the will of God in that situation, whatever the cost or consequence. "I will go in to the king," Esther affirmed, "and if I perish, I perish." God may want us to carry out some unpleasant task. It may involve confronting someone whom we would rather avoid or admitting something we have tried to hide, as it did with Esther. But if we know it to be the will of God, we must do it. And God will honor it. He did for Esther.

God worked in a marvelous way. In fact, he performed *a miracle for our encouragement.* First of all, he laid it on the king's heart to extend the golden sceptor, and Esther approached the throne. She spoke with quiet dignity rather than selfish demands or angry accusations. And instead of blurting out the problem, she invited Ahasuerus and Haman to dinner that evening. At dinner, she ignored the problem again, but rather invited them both to a second dinner the following evening. It was not that she was softening him up or trying to manipulate him. She was using good wisdom, and most husbands and wives could learn a lesson from Esther about how to speak and when to speak. Grace and tact are the key words in her approach.

God works in unusual ways. On the night between the banquets, Ahasuerus could not sleep. He asked for the record of his reign to be read to him. That would probably put him to sleep when nothing else could. In the record was the story of an assassination plot against him that Mordecai had discovered and exposed, for which act he had never been rewarded (Esth. 6:1-3). That incredible little episode set the scene for the events of the next day.

First, Haman was forced to honor Mordecai for his patriotism. And then it was time for Esther's second dinner party. As they feasted together, the king said to Esther, "What is your petition, Queen Esther? It shall be granted you. And what is your request? Even to half of the kingdom it shall be done." Esther's reply was brilliant: "If I have found favor in your sight, O king, and if it please the king, let my life be given me as my petition, and my people as my request; for we have been sold, I and my people, to be destroyed, to be killed and to be annihilated. Now if we had only been sold as slaves, men and women, I would have remained silent, for the trouble would not be commensurate with the annoyance to the king." The king was shocked. "Who is he, and where is he, who would presume to do thus?" And Esther put the finger on Haman, much to his horror (Esth. 7:1-6).

The results of that dinner party were awesome. Haman was hanged on the gallows he had built for Mordecai, and Mordecai was promoted to prime minister of Persia. And while the order to kill the Jews could not be rescinded, they were given permission to defend themselves against their enemies. Over 75,000 of their avowed adversaries were slain and God's people were delivered. It was nothing less than a miracle! But God loves to perform miracles for people who see themselves as part of his program, who view their circumstances as part of his appointment, and who live to do his will right where they are.

But there is one more thing we should notice in this narrative, and that is *a memorial for all time*. Both Mordecai and Esther were so grateful to God for his faithfulness that they sent letters to the Jews in all the provinces in Persia instructing them to celebrate the two days of their deliverance every year. They called it the Feast of Purim, from the word Pur, meaning "lot" or "dice." Haman had cast lots to determine the day the Jews should die (cf. Esth. 3:7; 9:24, 26). God turned it to a day of victory, and they were grateful to him for deliverance. The Jewish people celebrate the Feast of Purim to this day. It is a lasting memorial to God's faithfulness.

God is at work in our lives just as definitely and decisively as in Esther's. Our circumstances may not be all we would like them to be. But we can thank God for them anyway. They provide him with the opportunity to demonstrate his sovereign love and care, and they provide us with an opportunity to glorify him. Let us believe that he will work those circumstances together for good, then look for ways to serve him in them.

Let's talk it over

1. Why do you think God put the book of Esther in the Bible?
2. Recount some of the problems you have faced in the past that you now realize God has worked out for good.
3. What are the present circumstances in your life that you wish were different? What opportunities to glorify the Lord are provided by these circumstances? How can you serve the Lord in them?
4. How can you help each other handle the trying circumstances of life?
5. What did you learn from the relationship of Ahasuerus and Esther that will profit your relationship with each other?

10

IMPOSSIBLE THINGS DO HAPPEN
The Story of Zacharias and Elizabeth

THERE HAS BEEN a class consciousness in almost every culture in history, and the Jewish culture of Jesus' day was no exception. The upper class of that social structure consisted of the descendants of Aaron, the officiating priesthood. There were about 20,000 of them in and around Jerusalem at the time, and unfortunately many were proud, bigoted, overly indulgent, self-seeking men, religious only in those external matters that would impress other people. The priest in the parable of the Good Samaritan was a typical example. He considered himself to be above helping the unfortunate victim of a mugging and robbery.

But there were a few who were different and among them was an old priest named Zacharias, whose name means "the Lord remembers." Since the law of Moses insisted that a priest marry only a woman of highest reputation, Zacharias had chosen the daughter of another priest to be his wife. Not only was she a descendant of Aaron, but she bore the name of Aaron's own wife, Elisheba or Elizabeth, which means "the oath of God." Their names would spring alive with new significance before the sun set on their life together.

Look, first of all, at *their devout example*. "And they were both righteous in the sight of God, walking blamelessly in all the commandments and requirements of the Lord" (Luke 1:6). The lives of both Zacharias and Elizabeth were pleasing to God. They submitted to the will of God and obeyed the Word of God. And they did it "in the sight of God," that is, to exalt the Lord alone rather than to make a good showing before men. In that they were different from most of their contemporaries. They did not even care about the status that went with the priesthood. They lived in some obscure village in the hilly region south of Jerusalem rather than, as the other priests, in the elite section of the city itself, or in Jericho, the luxurious city of the palms. Their piety was no outward show; it was a heart relationship with the Lord. They cared more about what God thought of them than what men thought. And that, incidentally, is an important foundation on which to build a good marital relationship. The quality of our walk with God determines our ability to walk happily and harmoniously with each other. And that walk with him can only grow as we seek to please him rather than impress men.

That is not to say that Zacharias and Elizabeth had no problems. While many of our problems stem from our own sins, God does allow some to invade our lives for no other purpose but to help us grow. He wants them there, and no amount of obedience can possibly bring immunity from them. Zacharias and Elizabeth had one like that, and it was a big one. "And they had no child, because Elizabeth was barren, and they were both advanced in years" (Luke 1:7). It is difficult for us to imagine the intense stigma attached to childlessness for them. Many Jewish

Zacharias and Elizabeth

Rabbis insisted that it was an evidence of divine disfavor. While Zacharias and Elizabeth may have been righteous before God, some of their friends probably suspected them of serious secret sin. And there was no way to erase that blot. The phrase "advanced in years" meant at least sixty years of age, well beyond the time of childbearing. It was a hopeless situation.

Zacharias could have exonerated himself by divorcing Elizabeth. In their society, barrenness was a commonly accepted grounds for divorce. Zacharias could have gotten rid of her, married a younger woman, had children by his new wife, and gotten that damnable curse off his back. That was the route many other men would have taken. But not Zacharias. Instead he prayed (cf. Luke 1:13). He committed the situation to the one person who could do something about it. And while I cannot prove it, I would imagine that he prayed about it together with Elizabeth, and by that means ministered to her spiritual needs. He was also a man of the Word, as his famous "Benedictus" later revealed (cf. Luke 1:67-79). So he probably shared with his wife the great Old Testament Scriptures which would console her and encourage her in her plight.

That is a husband's responsibility as the spiritual leader in his marriage. The short time he has known the Lord may hinder him from fulfilling this role effectively at first, but as he grows in his understanding of the Word he will feel more comfortable encouraging his wife through the Word. Too often a wife has to drag her husband along spiritually; she coaxes, begs, and badgers him for every step he reluctantly takes in his spiritual growth. God does not want any of us trying to drag others along spiritually, but he does want husbands out in front, taking the spiritual lead and ministering to their wives and children in the things of Christ.

After Zacharias had committed his problem to God, he simply kept on with the job God had given him to do. He did not stop praying and bail out because his situation looked hopeless. And neither should we. Our God is the

God of the impossible! He delights in doing impossible things for us when he knows we shall give him the glory. It is so much easier to quit and run away from difficult circumstances, but that usually compounds the problem. God wants us to take our difficulties to him in prayer together, search the Word together for encouragement and direction, and then wait patiently for him to work.

Look next at *their most memorable day*. The day began with a great deal of excitement for Zacharias. "Now it came about, while he was performing his priestly service before God in the appointed order of his division, according to the custom of the priestly office, he was chosen by lot to enter the temple of the Lord and burn incense" (Luke 1:8, 9). It was his turn to minister before the golden altar of incense in the Holy Place, possibly for the first time in his priestly service. The priests had been divided into twenty-four courses by King David, and the order of Abijah, to which Zacharias belonged, was the eighth in line. Each course would be called to minister in the Temple on only two occasions during the entire year, each occasion lasting for one week. With nearly a thousand priests in each course, it becomes evident that entering the Holy Place and kindling the incense upon the golden altar was quite possibly a once-in-a-lifetime experience. But this was Zacharias' day.

First he would choose two special friends to assist him. One would reverently remove the ashes from the previous evening's sacrifice. Then the second would enter worshipfully and place new burning coals on the altar. Finally, Zacharias would enter the Holy Place alone, bearing the golden censer, and at the given signal he would spread the incense over the coals. As the incense kindled and a cloud of fragrance arose from the altar, the prayer of the worshipers outside would rise into the presence of God (cf. Luke 1:10). It was a beautifully symbolic experience of worship.

The ritual was finished now and it was time to leave the Holy Place. Suddenly an angel of the Lord appeared to

Zacharias, standing to the right of the altar of incense. The personal visit of an angel from God was a distinction that had been afforded only a few people in the history of the human race. And as you might imagine, it was a frightening experience. But immediately the angel spoke: "Do not be afraid, Zacharias, for your petition has been heard, and your wife Elizabeth will bear you a son, and you will give him the name John. And you will have joy and gladness, and many will rejoice at his birth" (Luke 1:13, 14). God can do impossible things, and that is exactly what he promised to do for Zacharias and Elizabeth. But their child was not to be just any ordinary child. He would be the forerunner of the Messiah predicted by the Prophet Malachi (Luke 1:15-17; cf. Mal. 3:1; 4:5, 6).

All this was too much for Zacharias to grasp. He had been praying for a son, but admittedly, his faith had been weakening. Now this Word from God—it was too good to be true. Before he had a chance to get his thoughts together, he blurted out, "How shall I know this for certain? For I am an old man, and my wife is advanced in years" (Luke 1:18). Zacharias was a man of God, but he was a man, and he had human weaknesses. God understands a weakness like this faltering faith. He is not exactly ecstatic about it, but he does understand it, and he goes to great lengths to stimulate and strengthen that faith. That is one reason he gave us his Word, and one reason he includes these great historic events in the Word. God's Word excites faith as we meditate on it and its application to our lives. "So faith comes from hearing, and hearing by the word of Christ" (Rom. 10:17).

Zacharias knew the Old Testament Scriptures. He knew how God had given a son to Sarah in her old age. But he did not think about that great Old Testament precedent at this moment of need. Even men of the Word may fail to appropriate it at times. But God did something very gracious for Zacharias to help him believe. He gave him a sign. "And behold, you shall be silent and unable to speak until the day when these things take place, because you did not believe my words, which shall be fulfilled in their proper time" (Luke 1:20). It was not very pleasant for him to lose his voice, and his hearing, as we later learn (cf. Luke 1:62). But I don't think Zacharias minded very much. His inability to speak and hear were God's confirmation of his Word, and they served to strengthen his faith in God's promise.

When Zacharias emerged from that Holy Place he was a different man. He had long been a godly man, but his encounter with the angel Gabriel left him with a new awareness of God's greatness, a new sense of his own unworthiness, and a strong, virile faith. When his week of priestly service was over, he hurried home to share with Elizabeth every detail of that memorable day, and they rejoiced together in God's grace.

"And after these days Elizabeth his wife became pregnant; and she kept herself in seclusion for five months" (Luke 1:24). That conception was a miracle. Impossible things do happen! And God is the same today as he always was (cf. Mal. 3:6; Josh. 1:17). He can solve our problems, and he put this story in his Word to prove it and to strengthen our faith.

Knowledge of this miracle stimulated the Virgin Mary's faith. God told her she would conceive a son without ever having relations with a man. That was rather hard to believe. But listen to the angel's reassuring message to her: "And behold, even your relative Elizabeth has also conceived a son in her old age; and she who was called barren is now in her sixth month. For nothing will be impossible with God" (Luke 1:36, 37). And with that amazing news, Mary responded, "Behold, the bondslave of the Lord; be it done to me according to your word" (Luke 1:38).

Some will invariably protest, "But you don't understand. My situation *is* impossible." "My husband will never change." "My wife will never learn." "We'll never get out of debt." "I'll never be well again." "My unsaved loved one will never come to know Christ." "This job will never improve." Listen to God's Word again: "For with God *nothing* shall be impossible." Believe that. Obey him. Then keep on keeping on.

The next major event in the lives of this godly couple was *their visit from Mary*, Elizabeth's young cousin from Nazareth, and through this visit we gain a little deeper insight into Elizabeth's character. It was in the sixth month of her pregnancy, and no sooner had Mary greeted her than her unborn baby leaped within her as if prompted by the Holy Spirit to salute the Son of God. Then, illuminated by that same Holy Spirit, she uttered these amazing words: "Blessed among women are you, and blessed is the fruit of your womb! And how has it happened to me, that the mother of my Lord should come to me?" (Luke 1:42, 43).

Her words are unusual for several reasons. For one thing, they reveal that she understood who Mary's child was. She calls Mary "the mother of my Lord." "My Lord" was a messianic title taken out of Psalm 110:1: "The Lord says to my Lord...." She acknowledged by divine revelation that Mary would give birth to the Messiah, the Son of God. But more amazing than that was her attitude toward Mary. While she knew that she herself had been honored of God, she realized that Mary had been infinitely more honored; in fact, more honored than any woman on earth. She did not even feel worthy of Mary's visit. Such utter humility and self-abasement are rare qualities. And although she was older than Mary and had every right to ask, "Lord, why didn't you choose me?" there was not one trace of jealously or self-seeking in her spirit. We can understand why God could bless her so richly.

Jealousy is a destructive emotion. It eats at our own souls, creates a hostile atmosphere in our homes, and ruins our relationships with our friends. But there is no jealousy in the life of one whose trust and hope are in God, as with Elizabeth. If we believe that God is doing what is best in our lives, and if we expect him to work out our impossible problems in his own time and in his own way, how can we be jealous of anybody else? We know that we are God's chosen vessels to fulfill his special purposes for us. We know that he is at work in our lives to accomplish his own good pleasure, and there can be no higher calling than doing his will. That confidence gives us an inner contentment, and contentment removes all jealousy. Learning to believe God will flush the biting jealousy out of our lives.

The last thing we want to notice in the lives of Zacharias and Elizabeth is *their miracle son*. I am sure they pored over the Old Testament Scriptures during the last few months of her pregnancy, reading every passage they could find concerning the Messiah and his forerunner. The nation had looked forward to this for centuries, and God had chosen this godly couple to be part of these thrilling events. Their excitement mounted daily, until "the time had come for Elizabeth to give birth, and she brought forth a son" (Luke 1:57).

As the custom was, their relatives and neighbors gathered to rejoice with them over this extraordinary event, and on the eighth day, at the child's circumcision, they tried to call him Zacharias after his father. But Elizabeth protested, "No indeed; but he shall be called John" (Luke 1:60). Why John? This was unheard of. Nobody in either of their families had ever been called John. Maybe this was just Elizabeth's folly. They had better ask Zacharias. "And they made signs to his father, as to what he wanted him called. And he asked for a tablet, and wrote as follows, 'His name is John.' And they were all astonished. And at once his mouth was opened and his tongue loosed, and he began to speak in praise of God" (Luke 1:62-64).

John means "The Lord is gracious." And how very gracious he had been to them. They merely asked for a son to carry on the family name and priesthood. God gave them the forerunner of the Messiah, a child upon whom the hand of God was evident from his earliest days, a man whom Jesus Christ would call the greatest among men (cf. Matt. 11:11). God does not always give according to our asking, and certainly not according to our deserving. He gives according to the riches of his grace. He does "exceeding abundantly beyond all that we ask or think" (Eph. 3:20). And he loves to do that for people who trust him and obey him, even in impossible situations.

The greatness of God's grace inspired Zacharias to utter a magnificent song of praise to God. He was filled with the Holy Spirit and said, "Blessed be the Lord God of Israel, for He has visited us and accomplished redemption for his people, and has raised up a horn of salvation for us in the house of David His servant—as He spoke by the mouth of His holy prophets from of old—salvation from our enemies, and from the hand of all who hate us; to show mercy toward our fathers, and to remember His holy covenant, the oath which He swore to Abraham our father" (Luke 1:68-73). That oath which God swore to Abraham is a reference to the Abrahamic Covenant in which God promised to bless the descendants of Abraham and make them a blessing to the whole earth. Many Jews were beginning to think God had forgotten his promise, that their national situation was hopeless. But Zacharias and Elizabeth never thought so. Together their names were a constant reminder that "Jehovah remembers his oath." And their miraculous experience proved it to be true. God not only remembers his promises, he keeps them!

Maybe you think the Lord has forgotten you in your hopeless situation. He hasn't. He does impossible things for people every day, and you may be next. So don't chafe and fret under the burden. Believe him. Keep on faithfully living for him and patiently waiting for him to work, just as Zacharias and Elizabeth did. While their names are not mentioned again after the birth of John, they have left us a lovely legacy of faith in the promises of God, the God of the impossible.

Let's talk it over

1. Zacharias and Elizabeth were "righteous in the sight of God." What things in your lives might make it difficult to apply that same statement to you? Would you be willing to covenant with God to seek his victory in these areas?

2. Why do you think so few Christian husbands take the spiritual lead in their homes? How can a wife encourage her husband in this matter without nagging?

3. Do you find traces of jealousy in your life periodically? If so, try recounting some of the special things God has done for you.

4. What promises in God's Word do you find difficult to believe? Memorize them, meditate on them, and claim them from God.

5. Is there a situation in your lives that seems impossible? Commit it to God in prayer together and ask him for the patience to live with it graciously until he changes it.

11

DO YOU TRUST ME?
The Story of Joseph and Mary

NAZARETH WAS a lovely little town snuggled in the hills overlooking the broad and fertile Plain of Esdraelon. It consisted primarily of some small white stone houses, a synagogue built on its highest knoll, and a marketplace at the entrance to the village. When the New Testament era dawned, its population seems to have numbered little more than one hundred, mostly farmers, but also some skilled craftsmen whose shops were found in the marketplace—a potter, a weaver, a dyer, a blacksmith, and a carpenter. The most momentous events of all human history were to involve the people associated with that humble carpenter shop in Nazareth.

The carpenter himself, a robust man in the prime of life named Joseph, was engaged to a young girl named Mary, probably still in her teen years. She was a girl upon whom God had bestowed much grace ("favored one," Luke 1:28). She was a sinner like all the rest of us, and she frankly admitted her low estate and her need for God's gracious salvation (cf. Luke 1:47, 48). But she had responded enthusiastically to his offer of forgiveness and had been daily appropriating his limitless grace for growth and godliness. She was greatly graced of God. And she lived with a sense of God's presence in her life. The Lord was with her (Luke 1:28). She enjoyed a beautiful moment-by-moment fellowship with God.

In spite of her intimate knowledge of God, however, it was a shocking and fearful experience when the angel Gabriel appeared to her: "Do not be afraid, Mary; for you have found favor with God. And behold, you will conceive in your womb, and bear a son, and you shall name Him Jesus. He will be great, and will be called the Son of the Most High; and the Lord God will give Him the throne of His father David; and He will reign over the house of Jacob forever; and His kingdom will have no end" (Luke 1:30-33). She questioned the angel, as well she might: "How can this be, since I am a virgin?" (Luke 1:34). And Gabriel explained the supernatural phenomenon that would accomplish this unbelievable feat. "The Holy Spirit will come upon you, and the power of the Most High will overshadow you; and for that reason the holy offspring shall be called the Son of God" (Luke 1:35). It was unbelievable, a miracle unsurpassed in human history, but it could be accomplished by the supernatural power of God, and Elizabeth's miraculous pregnancy was cited by the angel as evidence. Now the decision was Mary's: the decision to resist the will of God, or to become the willing servant through whom God could carry out his plan. And this decision is basically a matter of trust. As the story unfolds, we see first of all *Mary's trust in God*.

"What an honor," you say, "to be chosen as the mother of the Messiah. How could she decline?" Wait a minute. You may be saying that because you know the end of the story, but put yourself in Mary's place for a moment. Do you think anybody would really believe that this child was conceived of the Holy Spirit? Don't you think more people would conclude that Mary was covering up an escapade with some Roman soldier? The Roman district administrative center was only four miles northwest of Nazareth in Sepphoris, and Roman soldiers were frequently seen in the streets of Nazareth. Don't you think others might conclude that Mary and Joseph had gone too far in their relationship with each other and had disobeyed the law of God? In either case, was there not the possibility that Mary would be stoned for fornication?

And what about Joseph? He would know that he was not responsible for Mary's condition. What would he say? Would he still be willing to marry her? Was she willing to give him up if it would come to that? And what about the child? Would he not carry the stigma of illegitimacy with him throughout his entire life? In that brief moment in the angel's presence, all of Mary's dreams for the future flashed before her mind, and she could see every one of them shattered.

The question boils down to one thing for Mary: "Can I trust God to work out every problem I encounter if I submit myself to his will?" Mary had enjoyed an abundant supply of God's grace. She had reveled in her warm personal relationship with her Lord. But now he was asking her to face the greatest question in life for a believer walking in fellowship with him: "Mary, do you really trust me?"

Mary was a meditative woman. Twice we are told that she kept certain things and pondered them in her heart (cf. Luke 2:19, 51). But she did not take very much time to make up her mind here. She answered immediately, "Behold, the bondslave of the Lord; be it done to me according to your word" (Luke 1:38). Her decision was to submit to God's will and to trust him with the consequences. Submission to God's will almost always involves some risk. But God has promised to work all the details together for good, and we have no alternative but to believe it if we want to enjoy his peace and power.

The willingness to obey God and trust him with the consequences is a foundation stone in a good marriage. Every other man may neglect his wife to run around with the boys, chase after the latest fad, or play with his latest new acquisition. But God wants a Christian husband to put his wife above all else except Christ and love her as Christ loves the Church, trusting him to make the consequences far more satisfying than any hobby or recreational pursuit could be. Women's lib may sweep the day, but God wants a Christian wife to submit to her husband with a meek and quiet spirit, trusting God to enrich her marriage and fulfill her life through it. God may be asking us the same question he asked Mary: "Do you really trust me?"

Trust in God is only the beginning of a good marriage, however. There must also be a deep trust in each other, and no man has ever been asked to trust the girl he married more than the one in this story. Look then, at *Joseph's trust in Mary*. The chronology here is not clear. Whether or not Joseph knew of Mary's pregnancy before she departed for Elizabeth's home in Judea, we cannot be sure. But after her return three months later, the secret could no longer be hidden (cf. Luke 1:56 and Matt. 1:18). Did Mary tell Joseph of the miraculous conception? Did he find her story hard to believe even though he loved her deeply? Or did he accept it readily? Was his decision to break the engagement because he doubted her word, or was it because he considered himself unworthy to marry the mother of the Messiah, or was it because he thought Mary would have to raise the child in the Temple? His motive is not absolutely certain.

One thing is certain, however. There was a conflict raging in Joseph's soul. Whether he believed Mary's story or not, others would definitely not believe it, and he would live with gossip about an unfaithful wife for the rest of his life. But Joseph was both a godly man and a gracious man. Whatever he decided would reflect both godly wisdom and tender consideration for Mary. And although his heart was breaking, he was leaning toward quietly terminating the relationship and sparing her any public embarrassment (Matt. 1:19). At least he was open to the Lord's direction, though, and he was still prayerfully meditating on the right course of action when an angel of the Lord appeared to him in a dream and said, "Joseph, son of David, do not be afraid to take Mary as your wife; for that which has been conceived in her is of the Holy Spirit. And she will bear a Son; and you shall call His name Jesus, for it is He who will save His people from their sins" (Matt. 1:20, 21). Remember now, that this angel, unlike the one who came to Mary, appeared in a dream. Could it have been a dream inspired by wishful thinking, or was this really a message from God? We have no doubt that it was from God, for Scripture plainly says so. But Joseph did not know that. He may have doubted it at first. But a growing assurance began to sweep over him and trust solidified in his searching soul. The issue was settled—it mattered not what wagging tongues would say; Joseph believed! "And Joseph arose from his sleep, and did as the angel of the Lord commanded him, and took her as his wife; and kept her a virgin until she gave birth to a Son; and he called His name Jesus" (Matt. 1:24, 25). It was probably the greatest act of trust ever exhibited between a man and woman.

In reality, every marriage is a relationship of trust. When we stand at the altar and listen to our new mate promise to forsake all others and cleave to us alone, we believe it. When we hear his/her solemn promise to love us for better or worse until death parts us, we believe it. And because we believe it, we make the same promises in return and commit ourselves to a lifelong relationship. Trust in each other is another foundation stone in a good marriage, and it must grow as the years pass.

Trust is being able to tell our mates our innermost thoughts and feelings, believing they will never be used against us, believing we will be loved and accepted anyway, maybe even more so because of our honesty. Trust is feeling no anger or jealousy when we see our mates talking to someone of the opposite sex. Trust is believing our mates when they tell us where they have been or what they are thinking, or when they explain what they really meant by what they said.

Trust does put us at our husband's or wife's mercy. It makes us totally vulnerable, and we can get hurt that way! When we really believe someone and later find out that we have been deceived, it makes us feel foolish and humiliated. But what other choice do we have? Without trust there can be no relationship. So we ask God for the grace to keep on trusting, and we believe that God will use our trust to make our mate more trustworthy if need be. You see, it is not just the Lord asking that question of us. Our mate may also be asking, "Do you really trust me?"

The angel of God appeared to Joseph two more times, and those appearances reveal another element of trust in the nativity story—*Mary's trust in Joseph*. Joseph and Mary had completed the arduous trek to Bethlehem, and the ordeal of childbirth in a stable was now history. On the eighth day after Jesus' birth, they had him circumcised as the law required. Forty days after his birth, Mary offered her sacrifice of purification in the Temple. Then it seems as though they settled down in Bethlehem, possibly planning to make it their new home. Some time passed before the Magi arrived from Persia to worship the newborn king; and they found him in a house, not in the manger, as most nativity scenes suggest (Matt. 2:11).

The Magi had stopped in Jerusalem to find out where the Messiah should be born, and that alerted King Herod to this potential threat to his throne. That was the occasion of another message from an angel of the Lord to Joseph in a dream: "Arise and take the Child and His mother, and flee to Egypt, and remain there until I tell you; for Herod is going to search for the Child to destroy Him" (Matt. 2:13). While it was still night, Joseph gathered some of his belongings together, took Mary and Jesus, left for Egypt, and remained there until the death of Herod. This is worth noting. Mary is the more prominent figure in the

Christmas story, yet Joseph is the one to whom God gave his instructions. Joseph was the head of this family, and he was charged with protecting Jesus from Herod's wrath. Mary trusted his decision.

This was no vacation in the southland, mind you. This was a trip of about two hundred miles by foot or donkey, over mountains, wilderness, and desert, with a baby under two years of age. Most mothers can appreciate the degree of inconvenience that involved. I doubt whether Mary really wanted to go. If they had to leave Bethlehem, why not go back to Nazareth? Wouldn't they be just as safe there? But there is no indication in Scripture that Mary ever questioned Joseph's decision. And it happened again. After Herod's death, the angel spoke to Joseph in Egypt: "Arise and take the Child and His mother, and go into the land of Israel; for those who sought the Child's life are dead" (Matt. 2:20). Again, Joseph obeyed immediately; and again, Mary trusted Joseph to do the right thing.

As we saw in the lives of Abraham and Sarah, submission for a wife means trusting God to work through her husband to do what is best for her. And that includes trusting his decisions. But that is not exceptionally difficult when she knows her husband is acting in her best interest and is taking his directions from the Lord, as Joseph was. It seems that Joseph wanted to move back to Bethlehem in Judea, but was afraid to do so when he heard that Herod's son was reigning in his place. Again God gave him directions, and he returned to Nazareth where Mary's parents lived (Matt. 2:22, 23). Joseph made his decisions in accord with the will of God.

Men, we have no right to ask our wives to submit to us when we are arbitrarily expressing our own opinions, asserting our own selfish wills, or doing what is obviously best for us alone. But when we have clear directions from God that are best for all concerned and can share them fully with our wives, then they will be able to submit without hesitancy. We have an obligation to lead them in the path of God's choosing, not our own. We must learn to consult the Lord about every decision, spending time in prayer to seek his wisdom, searching the Word for his principles to guide us, and waiting for the settled assurance of his peace. And if there is an unquestionable desire to do God's will alone, regardless of our own personal preferences, he will protect us from making grievous mistakes that will bring unhappiness to our families. Then our wives will be free to follow our leadership with confidence and trust. Trust is not an easy and automatic response. It needs to be developed, particularly with those who have been deeply hurt. We can help others build a stronger trust in us by our own deepening commitment to the will of God. When they see that we are yielded to him, they will be able to trust us.

Let's talk it over

1. Try to put yourself in Mary's place, facing the awesome event of the virgin conception with all of its potential problems. How would you feel?

2. Have you at some point in your life given your future and all of its dreams to God to handle as he pleases? Do you need to reconfirm that decision?

3. Are there areas in your life that you have not yielded to God for fear of the consequences? Will you surrender them to him and ask him to help you trust him?

4. Try to put yourself in Joseph's place, facing marriage to a girl who is carrying a child presumably conceived by the Holy Spirit. How would you feel?

5. Can you think of areas of distrust in your relationship with each other? Share them with one another honestly, yet kindly. Have you been guilty of betraying your mate's trust? What can you do to increase your trust in each other?

6. For husbands: Are you ever guilty of expressing your own personal opinions and expecting your wife to submit? Have you learned to consult the Lord on every decision?

7. Are you helping others build a stronger trust in you by developing a stronger commitment to the will of God? How can you increase that commitment to do God's will?

12

LET'S BE HONEST
The Story of Ananias and Sapphira

"WE HAVE EACH OTHER, and that is all that matters," the love-struck couple boasted shortly after their wedding. But they were to find that it can never be so. No Christian husband and wife can be an island to themselves. They are part of a larger unit called the Body of Christ (Eph. 1:22, 23), the household of faith (Gal. 6:10), the household of God (Eph. 2:19). God's family is much broader than any single family unit, and we soon learn that our relationship to this larger spiritual family affects our relationship with each other as husbands and wives. Never was that more obvious than in the story of Ananias and Sapphira.

They lived in the days of the church's greatest purity and power. Consider, first of all, *the state of the church* in that exciting apostolic era. "And the congregation of those who believed were of one heart and soul; and not one of them claimed that anything belonging to him was his own; but all things were common property to them" (Acts 4:32). This is most amazing. The number of believers probably totaled five thousand or more by this time, and yet they were of one heart and one soul. The *heart* is sometimes used in Scripture to refer in a wider sense to the immaterial part of man's being, including both his spirit and his soul. But distinguished from the soul, as it is here, it would probably refer just to his spirit, the innermost facet of man's makeup, the center of his being to which God reveals himself and in which God dwells. Those early Christians sensed a spiritual bond at the deepest level of their lives. Their spirits were knit together in the cords of Christ's life and Christ's love. They knew they belonged to each other as brothers and sisters in Christ.

But Scripture goes on to say that they were of one soul as well, and that is something entirely different. The soul is the conscious life force in man, his personality, consisting of his mind, emotions, and will. This is the level on which he thinks his thoughts, senses his feelings, and makes his choices. This is the realm of experience. Those early Christians were not only one because of their position in Christ, but they were one in experience also. They thought alike, they had deep feelings for each other, and they made decisions that reflected their mutual care and concern. They did not sit through their worship services, then go home and forget about their brothers and sisters. Since their congregation was so very large, when they all met together in the court of the Temple, they also gathered in smaller units in homes to get to know each other, to grow in their love for one another, to care about one another's problems and minister to one another's needs (cf. Acts 2:46).

Their loving concern for one another went so far as to touch their wallets, and that is real care! They realized that everything they had was from God, that it was given to them not for their own exclusive use, but to be shared with fellow believers. There was no coercion involved. Any

believer was free to own property if he so chose, and no one
would think less of him for it. But most of them were selling
their material possesions and giving the money to the
apostles to be distributed to those who, in all probability,
had lost their jobs because of their faith. They were
sacrificing their own comforts and conveniences for the
good of all.

The result of this unselfish spirit was great power and
blessing on the entire church. "And with great power the
apostles were giving witness to the resurrection of the Lord
Jesus, and abundant grace was upon them all" (Acts 4:33).
A caring congregation is a strong congregation, for there
is dynamic energy in the genuine expression of God's love.
Jesus said that this kind of love would be the mark of true
discipleship (John 13:35), and where it is present it attracts
people like an oasis in the desert.

It attracted a couple named Ananias and Sapphira. They
were numbered among that powerful, caring community of
believers. Sapphira's name means "beautiful" or
"pleasant," the same name given to that precious stone of
deep purple blue, the sapphire. Ananias means "Jehovah is
gracious," and God certainly had been gracious to him.
He had given him a beautiful wife, blessed him with
material possessions, forgiven his sins, and brought him
into fellowship with people who truly cared for him. A man
couldn't ask for much more than that.

But Ananias did want more, and so did Sapphira. They
wanted more than acceptance; they wanted acclaim. They
wanted to be more than just members of the Body; they
wanted to be prominent members of the Body. They
wanted the praise of men. And that brings us, secondly, to
the sin of Ananias and Sapphira. Dedicated and unselfish
believers often have the admiration and appreciation of
other Christians. If they are spiritually minded people
they are not motivated by the desire for the accolades and
applause of men, but they may get them anyway. The
people in the early church who sold their possessions and
gave the money to the church probably received the

enthusiastic appreciation of the entire congregation. Barnabas was one who sacrificed everything (Acts 4:36, 37). It was no grandstand play with him. There was no trace of fleshly pride in it whatsoever. His only thought was the need of other Christians and the glory of God. But the acclaim was there. Ananias and Sapphira saw it and longed for it, and that is where their trouble began.

Coveting the plaudits of men was evidence enough that they were operating in the realm of the flesh rather than the Spirit. But that becomes even more obvious to us when we learn that their confidence for the future was in their bank account rather than in the Lord. They could not bear to do what the others were doing—give their substance totally to God and trust solely in his faithfulness to meet their needs. They had to have that money. And these two expressions of fleshliness, their desire for praise, and their confidence in material things, presented them with a difficult dilemma. How could they get the congratulations they craved from the congregation without laying everything on the altar of sacrifice? They finally came up with a solution. Fake it!

"But a certain man named Ananias, with his wife Sapphira, sold a piece of property, and kept back some of the price for himself, with his wife's full knowledge, and bringing a portion of it, he laid it at the apostles' feet" (Acts 5:1, 2). They collaborated on a plan to stash some of the money from the sale of their property in a safety deposit box for themselves and take the rest to the apostles. They would not necessarily say they were giving all of the money they received from the sale; they would just let everyone assume that. And *presto*, they would have instant acclaim as spiritual, self-sacrificing believers who had surrendered everything to Jesus Christ.

What was so wrong with their plan? They did not really lie to anybody, did they? They just gave the money and said nothing about what percentage of the total sale price it represented. They could not help what other people thought, could they? Evidently they could. Peter, with miraculous divine discernment, attributed their scheme to Satan and called it lying to the Holy Spirit (Acts 5:3). He explained that they were under no obligation to sell their property. And even after they sold it, they were under no obligation to give all the money to the church. But they *were* obligated to be honest (Acts 5:4). The major sin of Ananias and Sapphira was dishonesty, deceit, hypocrisy, pretense, presenting a false image of themselves, implying a greater spirituality than they actually possessed, letting people think more highly of them than what they knew was warranted. They were more interested in *appearances* than in *reality*. Peter said, "You have not lied to men, but to God" (Acts 5:4).

Have you ever wondered what kind of relationship Ananias and Sapphira had with each other? While they demonstrated a marvelous togetherness in their deceptive scheme, their hypocrisy could not help but have affected their marriage. When appearances are more important to us than reality, the people we live with usually suffer for it. We are careful to veil most of the expressions of the flesh before others, but safely behind the walls of our own homes, we have a tendency to let it all hang out—all the anger, all the temper, all the unkindness and inconsiderateness, all the selfish demands, all the pride, all the childish behavior. And as a result, many Christian homes are riddled with wrangling and strife. But when some concerned Christian who might be able to help us asks how things are going at home, we quickly reply, "Oh, just great, great. Yes sir, we're getting along better than we ever did." And we excuse our dishonesty by telling ourselves that what goes on in our home is a private matter, nobody's business but our own. But the dishonesty increases our burden of guilt, and the guilt leads to further defensiveness and irritability, and the irritability produces greater dissension and discord in the home. It's one of Satan's favorite traps.

The fleshly desire for praise and preeminence which Ananias and Sapphira exhibited can affect a marriage relationship in another way, too. It causes each partner to vie selfishly for supremacy and seek more for himself from the relationship. He gives of himself only to get something in return, and he usually keeps track of how much he gets. If he thinks he is coming out on the short end, he quarrels and complains until he gets what he thinks he deserves. Each partner is keeping score of who gives in the most, who gets the most attention, who shows the most appreciation, who has the most faults, or some other trivial area of contention. The need for each partner to come out looking better than his mate causes him to mask his true inner person, and so entrenches him more firmly in his wretched hypocrisy.

Let's be honest. Let's commit ourselves to absolute straightforwardness and transparency. That is the only way to break out of this devilish trap. When we admit our true feelings and motives to someone else, when we acknowledge our faults for what they are and ask someone to pray for us, it provides a helpful incentive to claim God's power to change. We know that someday that person will ask us how things are going and we will have to tell him honestly. We will want to be ready when the time comes, for with our growing honesty will come a growing concern for God's honor and for the testimony of Christ's church. So we will allow the Spirit of Jesus Christ to work in us to bring us into his likeness. Then we will be able to stop playing the game of putting on appearances. We will be real!

Husbands and wives can begin by being honest with each other. They can admit to one another what is going on inside them, then encourage one another and pray about each other's weaknesses. They also need to be honest with God. If their attitudes are wrong, even if they both share them alike, they must acknowledge them openly to the Lord and refuse to go on excusing them. Only then will they be able to grow spiritually. Ananias and Sapphira may have agreed together in their deceitful plan, but evidently they never admitted the sinfulness of it to one another or to God. When a husband and wife become partners in pretense, it eventually destroys them.

Look finally at *the significance of their discipline*. Peter did not call down judgment from heaven as some have supposed. He merely exposed Ananias' hypocrisy by the insight God gave him. "And as he heard these words, Ananias fell down and breathed his last" (Acts 5:5). It was the disciplinary hand of God. "And the young men arose and covered him up, and after carrying him out, they buried him" (Acts 5:6). We do not know how they got Ananias buried without Sapphira knowing about it, but bodies had to be buried quickly in those days and maybe they could not find Sapphira at the moment. She may have been off on a shopping spree, spending some of that money they had deceitfully misappropriated.

Three hours later she came in looking for her husband, oblivious to what had transpired. Peter gave her an opportunity to be honest. "Tell me whether you sold the land for such and such a price?" he asked, quoting the amount which Ananias had brought to him. Sapphira chose to perpetuate the same false front her husband had initiated. Without a moment's hesitation she answered, "Yes, that was the price" (Acts 5:8). And Peter declared that she would experience the same fate which Ananias had suffered.

We cringe at this extreme illustration of divine discipline. We may even be tempted to accuse God of overreacting with undue harshness. Why did he do it? He does not seem to act that way now. And we can be grateful for that! But those days were different. They were the formative days of the church. Up until that time there had been no such crass exhibition of fleshliness, and God loathed the day it would permeate the church. From the very outset, he wanted it known how strongly he feels about hypocrisy, and he wanted it known for all time. That is why he put this account into his Word.

Phony spirituality is contagious. It spreads. When one Christian sees another Christian getting away with it, he finds it easier to try it himself. And for every member who operates in the power of the flesh rather than the Spirit, for every one who lives for the praise of men rather than for the glory of God, the effectiveness of Christ's church is reduced so much the more. Had God permitted Ananias and Sapphira to continue their charade, it would have destroyed the witness of the early church. He had to act decisively.

Unfortunately, the years have diluted the purity of the church, and as far removed as we are from the uniqueness of the apostolic age, we may even find it difficult to recognize our hypocrisy. We understand hypocrisy to be a deliberate and calculated effort to deceive, as it was with Ananias and Sapphira, and we may not be consciously doing that. We may simply have fallen into the unconscious habit of protecting our saintly image, covering our carnality, keeping people from knowing what is going on in our hearts and in our homes. That is usually easier than committing ourselves totally to Christ and letting him live through us to make the changes he wants to make. This form of hypocrisy has become a way of life in the church of Jesus Christ today, and may be the reason we are not making any greater impact on our godless society.

A penetrating question lingers in our minds after we have drawn the curtain on the life of Ananias and Sapphira. Which is really more important to us—to maintain the appearance of spirituality, or genuinely to be what God wants us to be? Cultivating the appearance alone leads to death—death to further spiritual growth, death to usefulness in the family of God, and death to a growing relationship with each other as husbands and wives. But the Spirit of God can use an honest openness, on the other hand, to produce in us the life of Christ, and that means abundant life, abiding joy, and abounding blessing.

Ananias and Sapphira

Let's talk it over

1. How could Ananias and Sapphira have avoided the trap of deceit into which they fell?

2. What are Christians generally most prone to mask from each other?

3. Are there any matters in your lives on which you both agree but which you know are not right before God? What does God want you to do about them?

4. What are husbands and wives most likely to conceal from each other?

5. What are the risks of husbands and wives being transparent with each other?

6. How approachable are you? Ask your mate whether or not it is easy to be honest with you. Why or why not?

7. Is there any sign that either of you is seeking the supremacy in your relationship (such as "keeping score")? How can you avoid this tendency?

13

SIDE BY SIDE
The Story of Aquila and Priscilla

IN THE YEAR 52 A.D. the Roman emperor Claudius issued an edict expelling all Jews from the city of Rome. It seems, from what the Roman historian Suetonius says, that they were persecuting their Christian neighbors and causing considerable disturbance in the city. Claudius cared little about the reason for the trouble, and even less about who the guilty parties were. He knew they were Jews, and that was enough; so all Jews were uprooted from their homes and banished from Rome, the innocent along with the guilty.

That was when a Jew named Aquila, who had migrated to Rome from the province of Pontus on the Black Sea, packed his belongings, bid farewell to his friends, and embarked for the city of Corinth. By his side was his faithful wife, Priscilla. We do not know for certain whether she was Jewish or

Roman, nor are we sure whether or not they were both Christians at the time. But one thing we do know—they were together. In fact, they were always together. One's name never occurs without the other.

For one thing, *they made their living together*. "For by trade they were tent-makers" (Acts 18:3). Every Jewish boy in New Testament times was taught some kind of trade. Since tents were such a prominent part of Hebrew life, Aquila's parents chose to have their son learn this practical means of earning his livelihood. Their tents were made of rough goat's hair fabric which took great skill to cut and sew properly. Aquila had acquired that skill and later taught it to his wife, and she happily assisted him in his business.

Not every husband and wife can work together like this. It takes a mature relationship to work closely under the kind of pressure a job sometimes generates. But that is evidently the kind of relationship Aquila and Priscilla had. They were not only mates and lovers, they must have been good friends and companions. They had to be willing to give to each other more than they tried to take. They had to be able to accept suggestions as readily as they offered them. They enjoyed being together and working together. They were inseparable, and they were equals.

So when they arrived in Corinth, they scoured the marketplace together for a small open-air shop to rent, and proceeded to set up their tentmaking business. The timing was obviously of God, for no sooner had they gotten settled down in their shop than another Jewish tentmaker arrived in town fresh from an evangelistic crusade in Athens, the Apostle Paul. Whenever he entered a new city, he would stroll through the marketplace looking for opportunities to talk about Jesus, looking for indications of God's direction for future ministry, and, of course, looking for work to sustain him as he ministered. It was inevitable that he would amble into the tentmaking shop of Aquila and Priscilla. Scripture tells the story like this: "After these things he left Athens and went to Corinth. And he found a certain Jew named Aquila, a native of Pontus, having

134

recently come from Italy with his wife Priscilla, because
Claudius had commanded all the Jews to leave Rome. He
came to them, and because he was of the same trade, he
stayed with them and they were working; for by trade they
were tent-makers" (Acts 18:1-3).

Their affinity for each other was instantaneous, and a
deep and lasting friendship was born that day. Paul came to
work with them in their shop, and even lived with them in
their home during his stay in Corinth. If they had not
known Christ before this, they certainly met him now, for
no one could spend time in Paul's presence and not be
infected by his contagious and enthusiastic love for his
Savior. These two who lived together, worked together,
and suffered exile together, came to know and love Jesus
Christ together, and it made their marriage complete. Now
they were one in Christ, and his love made a good marriage
even better. That may be just the thing your marriage
needs. If either one of you has never placed your faith in
the sacrifice which Christ made for your sins, your marriage
cannot be complete. True oneness can only be found in
Christ.

From the day Aquila and Priscilla met the Savior, *they
grew in the Word together.* No doubt they went with Paul to
the synagogue each Sabbath day as he reasoned with the
Jews and Greeks and encouraged them to place their trust
in Christ for salvation (Acts 18:4). Not everyone received his
testimony. Some resisted and blasphemed. So he withdrew
from the synagogue and began teaching in the house of
Titus Justus next door. And God blessed his ministry. Even
the chief ruler of the synagogue came to know Christ. "And
he settled there a year and six months, teaching the word of
God among them" (Acts 18:11). Think of it, eighteen
months of intensive Bible study under the greatest Bible
teacher in the early church. How Aquila and Priscilla must
have grown!

And after the lessons were over, the three of them
probably went home together and sat up into the early
hours of the morning talking about the Lord and his Word.

They grew to love God's Word. And although they worked long and hard running their shop, making and repairing tents, maintaining a home and caring for their distinguished guest, they always found time for serious Bible study. Sharing the Word together strengthened their love for each other and their spirit of togetherness.

This is exactly what many Christian marriages lack. Husbands and wives need to open the Word together. That is not difficult to do in a pastor's home. When I am preparing a message, I often talk to my wife about it and get her thoughts on the passage I am studying. If she is preparing a lesson, she may come to get my help in understanding a particular verse, and we find ourselves sharing the Word together. But it may be more difficult at your house, especially if you have never done it. Teaching a Sunday school class and sharing the preparation with each other might be a comfortable way to begin. Reading and discussing a Bible-centered devotional guide would be profitable. Reading through a book of the Bible together will allow God to speak to our lives. However we make use of it, God's Word is one necessary ingredient for enriching our relationship with each other.

The events that follow in the account of the Acts reveal how thoroughly Aquila and Priscilla learned God's Word. When Paul left Corinth for Ephesus, they accompanied him, and he left them there when he embarked for his home church in Antioch (Acts 18:18-22). The move was providential, for while Paul was gone "a certain Jew named Apollos, an Alexandrian by birth, an eloquent man, came to Ephesus; and he was mighty in the Scriptures. This man had been instructed in the way of the Lord; and being fervent in spirit, he was speaking and teaching accurately the things concerning Jesus, being acquainted only with the baptism of John; and he began to speak out boldly in the synagogue" (Acts 18:24-26).

Aquila and Priscilla went to hear him and were deeply impressed by his sincerity, his love for God, his knowledge of the Old Testament Scriptures, and his brilliant oratorical

ability. He could be mightily used in the service of
Jesus Christ, but his message was deficient. All he knew
beyond the Old Testament was the message of John the
Baptist, which merely looked forward to the coming
Messiah. "But when Priscilla and Aquila heard him, they
took him aside and explained to him the way of God more
accurately" (Acts 18:26). They lovingly and patiently
rehearsed the life and ministry of Jesus Christ on earth, his
sacrificial and substitutionary death on Calvary's cross
for the sins of the world, his victorious resurrection from the
tomb and glorious ascension into heaven, the necessity for
personal salvation from sin by faith in his finished work, the
coming of the Holy Spirit at Pentecost, and the birth of
the Body of Christ, and other great New Testament
doctrines.

Aquila and Priscilla may not have been accomplished
public speakers, but they were diligent students of the
Word, and they loved to share it with others. They were
even willing to invest the time necessary to take one young
man under their spiritual care and pour into his life the
things of Christ. Apollos had a keen mind and a quick
understanding. He absorbed the truth they taught him and
made it a part of his life and ministry. And as a result of
this encounter with Aquila and Priscilla, he became an
effective servant of God whom some of the Corinthians later
placed on a level with Peter and Paul (1 Cor. 1:12).

Some of us will never be powerful preachers, but we can
be faithful students of the Word, and our homes can be
open to people whose hearts are hungry to hear the Word.
We may have the joyous privilege of nurturing a young
Apollos who someday will have a wide and powerful
ministry for Jesus Christ.

Aquila and Priscilla not only made their living together
and grew in the Word together, *they served the Lord together*.
We know it from what we have already seen, but there is
another facet of their Christian service that bears mention.
When Paul left Antioch on his third missionary journey, he
traveled through Asia Minor by land and returned to

Ephesus, where he remained teaching the Word of God for approximately three years (cf. Acts 20:31). During that period of time, he wrote his first letter to the Corinthians and said, "The churches of Asia greet you. Aquila and Prisca greet you heartily in the Lord, with the church that is in their house" (1 Cor. 16:19).

When they were just getting started in business in Corinth their home was probably not big enough to hold all the Christians, so the house of Titus Justus was used. But now it looks as though God had blessed them materially, and they were using their resources in Ephesus for his glory. Their home was a meeting place for the Ephesian church.

And that would not be the last time their home served that purpose. When Paul left Ephesus for Greece, they evidently believed God was directing them back to Rome. Claudius was dead now, so the move seemed safe, and Rome surely needed a gospel witness. So off they went! Paul wrote his epistle to the Romans from Greece on that third missionary journey, and he said, "Greet Prisca and Aquila, my fellow-workers in Christ Jesus, who for my life risked their own necks, to whom not only do I give thanks, but also all the churches of the Gentiles; also greet the church that is in their house" (Rom. 16:3-5). They had hardly gotten to Rome and already there was a church meeting in their house. Churches in New Testament times could not afford to own land and build buildings, nor would it have been wise to do so if they could, in view of the continual pressure and persecution. They met in homes. And the home of Aquila and Priscilla was always open to people who wanted to learn more about Christ, and for Christians who wanted to grow in the Word.

While we have church buildings, there is no substitute for the home as a center for evangelism and spiritual nurture in the community. Some Christians conduct evangelistic dinners, where they invite unsaved friends to hear an outstanding personal testimony. Many dedicated women use coffee cup evangelism, establishing close friendships with their neighbors and sharing Christ with them over the kitchen table. Home Bible classes can be an effective tool for reaching the lost or getting believers growing in the Word. Young people have profited greatly by adults who have opened their homes to youth groups. The possibilities for using our homes to serve the Lord are unlimited. This might be a good thing for husbands and wives to discuss and pray about together.

There was one short statement in the greeting in the Book of Romans that we cannot afford to pass over lightly, however: "Who for my life risked their own necks, to whom not only do I give thanks, but also all the churches of the Gentiles." We do not know what Paul was referring to, nor when it happened, but somewhere, somehow, Aquila and Priscilla together endangered their own lives to save Paul's. And for that we also can give thanks to God. Our knowledge of divine truth would be incomplete without the epistles which God inspired him to write. His two friends were willing to give everything in the service of the Savior, even their lives.

Aquila and Priscilla are mentioned one more time in the New Testament, in the last chapter of the last book the Apostle Paul wrote. It had been sixteen years since Paul first met them at Corinth, and now he was in a Roman prison for the second time. His death at the hands of the emperor Nero was imminent, and he was writing the last paragraph of his long and fruitful life. "Greet Prisca and Aquila, and the household of Onesiphorus" (2 Tim. 4:19). He is thinking of his dear friends who were then back in Ephesus where Timothy was ministering, possibly having left Rome to escape Nero's latest outburst of persecution against Christians. It was just a brief and simple greeting, using the shorter form of Priscilla's name that we have seen in several other passages. But Paul wanted to be remembered to them in the last hours of his life.

There is an interesting observation to be made from that short verse, however. Priscilla's name appears before Aquila's. In fact, her name is first in four out of the six biblical references to them. And that is unusual! Most references to husbands and wives in the Bible place the man first. Why the switch? Several explanations have been suggested, but the most reasonable one seems to be that Priscilla was the more gifted of the two and often took the more prominent role. Yet it appears that that never affected their love for one another, their understanding of each other, nor their ability to work together.

It does not always happen that way. Some husbands feel threatened because their wives are more knowledgeable or capable than they are, and in order to avoid embarrassment and save face they sometimes become spiritual dropouts. It is easier for them not to show up at all than to have their wives outshine them. Others become overbearing and belligerent in an attempt to establish their position of authority.

In some cases the wives are to blame. They seem to have something to prove, competing with their husbands for the spotlight, grasping after authority and preeminence. It is no wonder their husbands feel threatened. God's order of authority in marriage never changes. Although the wife may be more intelligent and resourceful than her husband, God still wants her to look to him as her leader. That is not always easy for an extremely talented woman to do, but Priscilla did it. She was not competing with Aquila. She was just using her God-given abilities, as a helpmeet to her husband for the glory of God. I am sure Aquila thanked God for her many times and accepted her wise counsel on many occasions. She was one of the world's truly liberated women, for there is no freedom that brings more joy and satisfaction than the freedom of obeying God's Word.

Let's talk it over

1. Are you looking for opportunities to share Christ wherever you go, as Paul did? Do those who spend time with you become

infected with your love for Christ? How can you improve this area of your life?

2. What spiritual contribution are you making to the lives of others? What else could you be doing to share God's Word with others?

3. How could you use your home more effectively to serve the Lord?

4. Are you sharing the Word of God with each other? Discuss what kind of mutual Bible study you think will work best for you, then covenant to do it regularly together.

5. For husbands: Does it bother you when your wife outshines you? How does God want you to behave toward her on those occasions?

6. For wives: Are you threatening your husband by striving to prove your superiority in certain areas? Do you seek praise from others at his expense? How can you avoid these pitfalls?

7. Are there occasions when you feel that your mate undermines you in public? Share this with each other and discuss how it can be avoided.

8. If you and your mate were considering working together in a business, what problems would you foresee arising? What could you do now to avoid those problems?

9. How can you demonstrate more fully the equality you share in Christ as husband and wife?